OPPOSING
VIEWPOINTS®
SERIES

Professional Athletes

Other Books of Related Interest:

At Issue

Are Players' Unions Good for Professional Sports Leagues?

Introducing Issues with Opposing Viewpoints

Athletes and Drug Use

Issues That Concern You

Exercise and Fitness

"Congress shall make no law . . . abridging the freedom of speech, or of the press."

First Amendment to the US Constitution

The basic foundation of our democracy is the First Amendment guarantee of freedom of expression. The Opposing Viewpoints series is dedicated to the concept of this basic freedom and the idea that it is more important to practice it than to enshrine it.

Professional Athletes

Margaret Haerens and Lynn M. Zott, Book Editors

GREENHAVEN PRESS
A part of Gale, Cengage Learning

GALE
CENGAGE Learning·

Detroit • New York • San Francisco • New Haven, Conn • Waterville, Maine • London

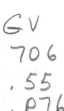 

GALE
CENGAGE Learning·

Elizabeth Des Chenes, *Director, Content Strategy*
Cynthia Sanner, *Publisher*
Douglas Dentino, *Manager, New Product*

LIBRARY OF CONGRESS CATALOGING-IN-PUBLICATION DATA

Professional athletes / Margaret Haerens and Lynn M. Zott, book editors.
     pages cm. -- (Opposing viewpoints)
     Includes bibliographical references and index.
     ISBN 978-0-7377-6068-2 (hardcover) -- ISBN 978-0-7377-6069-9 (pbk.)
     1. Athletes--Conduct of life. I. Haerens, Margaret.
     GV706.55.P76 2013
     796.01--dc23

                                                                    2013002125

Printed in the United States of America
1 2 3 4 5   17 16 15 14 13

Contents

Chapter 3: Should Limitations Be Placed on Athletes' Free Expression?

Chapter 4: What Are Some Controversies Surrounding Professional Athletes?

Why Consider Opposing Viewpoints?

> "The only way in which a human being can make some approach to knowing the whole of a subject is by hearing what can be said about it by persons of every variety of opinion and studying all modes in which it can be looked at by every character of mind. No wise man ever acquired his wisdom in any mode but this."
>
> *John Stuart Mill*

In our media-intensive culture it is not difficult to find differing opinions. Thousands of newspapers and magazines and dozens of radio and television talk shows resound with differing points of view. The difficulty lies in deciding which opinion to agree with and which "experts" seem the most credible. The more inundated we become with differing opinions and claims, the more essential it is to hone critical reading and thinking skills to evaluate these ideas. Opposing Viewpoints books address this problem directly by presenting stimulating debates that can be used to enhance and teach these skills. The varied opinions contained in each book examine many different aspects of a single issue. While examining these conveniently edited opposing views, readers can develop critical thinking skills such as the ability to compare and contrast authors' credibility, facts, argumentation styles, use of persuasive techniques, and other stylistic tools. In short, the Opposing Viewpoints Series is an ideal way to attain the higher-level thinking and reading skills so essential in a culture of diverse and contradictory opinions.

In addition to providing a tool for critical thinking, Opposing Viewpoints books challenge readers to question their own strongly held opinions and assumptions. Most people form their opinions on the basis of upbringing, peer pressure, and personal, cultural, or professional bias. By reading carefully balanced opposing views, readers must directly confront new ideas as well as the opinions of those with whom they disagree. This is not to argue simplistically that everyone who reads opposing views will—or should—change his or her opinion. Instead, the series enhances readers' understanding of their own views by encouraging confrontation with opposing ideas. Careful examination of others' views can lead to the readers' understanding of the logical inconsistencies in their own opinions, perspective on why they hold an opinion, and the consideration of the possibility that their opinion requires further evaluation.

Evaluating Other Opinions

To ensure that this type of examination occurs, Opposing Viewpoints books present all types of opinions. Prominent spokespeople on different sides of each issue as well as well-known professionals from many disciplines challenge the reader. An additional goal of the series is to provide a forum for other, less known, or even unpopular viewpoints. The opinion of an ordinary person who has had to make the decision to cut off life support from a terminally ill relative, for example, may be just as valuable and provide just as much insight as a medical ethicist's professional opinion. The editors have two additional purposes in including these less known views. One, the editors encourage readers to respect others' opinions—even when not enhanced by professional credibility. It is only by reading or listening to and objectively evaluating others' ideas that one can determine whether they are worthy of consideration. Two, the inclusion of such viewpoints encourages the important critical thinking skill of objectively evaluating an author's credentials and bias. This evaluation will illuminate an author's reasons for taking a particular stance on an issue and will aid in readers' evaluation of the author's ideas.

It is our hope that these books will give readers a deeper understanding of the issues debated and an appreciation of the complexity of even seemingly simple issues when good and honest people disagree. This awareness is particularly important in a democratic society such as ours in which people enter into public debate to determine the common good. Those with whom one disagrees should not be regarded as enemies but rather as people whose views deserve careful examination and may shed light on one's own.

Thomas Jefferson once said that "difference of opinion leads to inquiry, and inquiry to truth." Jefferson, a broadly educated man, argued that "if a nation expects to be ignorant and free . . . it expects what never was and never will be." As individuals and as a nation, it is imperative that we consider the opinions of others and examine them with skill and discernment. The Opposing Viewpoints series is intended to help readers achieve this goal.

David L. Bender and Bruno Leone,
Founders

Introduction

"You can't enter the sports arena and run your mouth without repercussions. Both college and professional sports have come to serve as the country's moral compass when it comes to hateful and hurtful speech. Of course, it's somewhat surprising that sports leagues should be moral guides given how many National Football League players were arrested in 2006 alone. But time after time, it's been proved: when it comes to sports, you better watch your mouth."

—Evan Weiner,
"Is Sports the Third Rail of American Society?,"
NewJerseyNewsroom.com,
October 19, 2010

"This new age of athletes are willing to use their social status to influence the political and cultural landscape. Change is constant, but growth is optional. . . . You may not always agree with the stance of your favorite athlete, but at least these days they have an opinion, and it seems they are willing to let the world know.

—LaMar C. Campbell,
Detroit Lions cornerback, 1998–2004,
"Pro Athletes Ignore Backlash, Show True Political Colors,"
CNN.com, September 21, 2012

On April 9, 2012, a huge baseball controversy erupted when *Time* magazine published an interview with Ozzie Guillén, at the time the new manager of the Miami Marlins, a Major League Baseball (MLB) team. During a rambling interview, Guillén touched on a number of unrelated topics, including sports psychology, bullfighting, and how his penchant for honesty had irritated his wife. Then the Marlins manager turned to politics. "I love Fidel Castro," he blurted out. "I respect Fidel Castro. You know why? A lot of people have wanted to kill Fidel Castro for the last 60 years, but that mother------ is still here."

With those words, Guillén found himself in one of the biggest controversies of his career, and Guillén is no stranger to controversy. An accomplished player and coach, as well as one of the best baseball managers in the major leagues, he led the Chicago White Sox to win the World Series in 2005 and was voted the American League (AL) Manager of the Year. As talented as Guillén was on the field managing players, he seemed to run into trouble off the field. After the White Sox won the 2005 World Series, Guillén received criticism when he skipped the team's visit to the White House because he had already planned a vacation with his family. Months later, Guillén was forced to apologize when he hurled an antigay slur at a baseball reporter. In 2010 he sharply condemned Arizona's harsh immigration law and asserted that Asian players were better treated than Latino players in professional baseball. Guillén also had a history of praising American-bashing politicians, generating heat with his positive comments about Hugo Chávez, the president of his native country of Venezuela and a vocal critic of US foreign policy.

But it was Guillén's praise for the Cuban dictator Fidel Castro that angered the South Florida community—and in fact, many Americans. For decades, Castro had reigned as the brutal dictator of Cuba, an island off the coast of South Florida, after overthrowing the US-backed Cuban president

Fulgencio Batista in 1959. The Castro regime nationalized industry; eliminated freedom of the press; and jailed, tortured, and killed dissidents and political enemies. Human rights organizations have widely castigated Castro's poor record of human rights, accusing him of perpetrating horrible abuses against his people. Hundreds of thousands of dissidents were forced to flee Cuba—leaving behind their homes and families—to escape Castro's harsh economic and political policies. Over the years, many of these exiles had settled in South Florida and were actively trying to effect political change in Cuba. To those with personal experience of Castro's brutality and injustice, Guillén's comments were particularly painful and completely outrageous.

However, Castro's resiliency and Cuba's resistance to American influence have also inspired the admiration of many in Latin America and around the world. Some supporters laud Castro as a brave anti-imperialist who introduced free health care and initiated social and economic reforms to address income inequality and correct the excesses of capitalism.

Guillén's comments ignited a firestorm of controversy across the United States, especially among members of the Miami community, many of whom are children and grandchildren of Cuban exiles—or exiles themselves. Guillén was attacked as a Communist, a traitor, and an eccentric who didn't know when to keep his mouth shut. Outraged fans organized protests calling for his firing. A candidate for mayor of Miami hired a plane to circle Marlins Park with a banner referring to Guillén's betrayal of the Cuban community. Another candidate suggested that Guillén was in danger and should leave Miami for a while until things cooled down.

The Miami Marlins acted quickly and decisively to quell the public relations disaster. Guillén was suspended without pay for five games. On April 10, he apologized to the Marlins and their fans for his comments in a press conference. "I'm here on my knees to apologize," Guillén said. "It was a personal mistake of the thing I had in my mind and what I said. What I wanted to say in Spanish, I said in English in a wrong way."

He also underscored his own involvement in the community and his determination to make things right. "I live in Miami," he said. "My family's in Miami. I will do everything, and I'm willing to do everything, to try to make it better. We'll help the Cuban community, the Latino community, like I always do. And I hope I get better and people understand my situation. But I am willing to do everything in my power— and the Marlins' power—to help this community like I always do."

The controversy over Guillén's comments sparked a debate over the limits to free speech in sports. Many observers pointed out that no matter how offensive Guillén's comments were, they were protected under the US Constitution as free speech. They suggested that the Marlins capitulated to public pressure and were victims of a culture too concerned with political correctness.

Others argued that the Miami Marlins organization not only had the right, but the duty, to respond to fans' concerns and demands. Baseball Commissioner Bud Selig, in an April 2012 article on ESPN.com, maintained that Guillén's remarks "have no place in our game" and were "offensive to an important part of the Miami community and others throughout the world." Several critics even contended that Guillén had gone too far, and that the Marlins should fire him for his comments.

Despite the firestorm, Guillén still had the support of the Marlins. "We believe in him," said David Samson, the team president, in the ESPN.com article. "We believe in his apology. We believe everybody deserves a second chance."

Nevertheless, at the end of the 2012 season Guillén was fired by the Marlins. Officially, the move was blamed on the team's poor season—the Marlins finished last in their division, the National League (NL) East. ESPN baseball analyst Jayson Stark argued that Guillén's Castro comments also played a major role in his firing. "It destroyed one of Ozzie's greatest selling points as a manager of their team," he contended in an October 2012 article on ESPN.com. "Their goal was to try to position themselves not just as South Florida's team and South Beach's team, but as Latin America's team. And think about where the ballpark is located. It's located in Little Havana. For Ozzie to come out and say anything even remotely complimentary to Fidel Castro when the ballpark is literally in the midst of Little Havana was a nightmare. It was their worst nightmare."

The authors of the viewpoints presented in *Opposing Viewpoints: Professional Athletes* explore issues relating to professional athletes in the following chapters: What Is the Role of Professional Athletes in Society?, How Should Pro Sports Treat Performance-Enhancing Drugs and Injuries?, Should Limitations Be Placed on Athletes' Free Expression?, and What Are Some Controversies Surrounding Professional Athletes? The information in this volume provides insights into a number of topics related to professional athletes, including the role of athletes in society; the approach to steroids, concussions, and public religious expression; and societal attitudes toward openly gay athletes and athletes who become politicians after their playing careers have ended.

OPPOSING VIEWPOINTS® SERIES

CHAPTER 1

What Is the Role of Professional Athletes in Society?

Chapter Preface

In the 2005 Major League Lacrosse (MLL) draft, the Boston Cannons drafted a talented young goaltender out of Dartmouth College named Andrew Goldstein. Although top college players are drafted every year by professional teams in every major American sport, the Boston Cannons had done something no other team had done: It had drafted the first openly gay male athlete to play in professional sports in the United States. This was a major milestone for both professional sports and for LGBT (lesbian, gay, bisexual, and transgender) sports history.

As a college student and athlete at Dartmouth, Goldstein had come out to his team and was widely accepted by his teammates. In an article written for Discourse, a website for gay athletes, Goldstein reflected on how that positive experience impacted his mental state and performance on the field. "I just wanted a chance to go out there and play the sport that I love without having to hide my sexuality from my teammates who are most of my closest friends," he stated. "The world of sports gives me a chance to both stand out and fit in all at the same time. When Saturday games come around, I get to perform on the field in front of all of the fans and show off my talents. But when the game is over, it's the guys telling me that I had a good game who really make me feel accepted. I am just one of the guys, part of a team, no matter what my sexual orientation is. In the world of sports, where the mental side is just as important as the physical, I can't understand how an athlete could be expected to play freely and to the most of his or her abilities holding this whole part of life behind."

Goldstein's experience playing professional lacrosse was also very positive. He contends that in his two-year career with two different teams, he never once heard slurs or was insulted on the basis of his sexuality. His teammates were open and accepting, and the officials on the Boston Cannons and Long Island Lizards were very supportive. Scott Niess, a team spokesman, observed that Goldstein's sexuality was irrelevant. "It isn't an issue with us. We're a professional lacrosse team who drafted Andrew for his skills in the cage. His teammates are all professional about it, and he is treated like any other player by us."

Drafting an openly gay player was an important achievement in professional sports. However, commentators quickly pointed out that it happened in the minor sport of lacrosse—and not in one of the four major US professional sports: football, baseball, basketball, or hockey. As Goldstein said in an article, "I can't say my experience in this small, fringe sport is equivalent to what would happen in one of these big leagues. All I can say is it wasn't an issue and there was no reason for it to be an issue other than the issue itself."

In the four major US professional sports, several men have come out to the public once their playing careers had ended, citing a concern over how they would be treated by team officials, teammates, or fans if their sexuality were known while they were still playing. During their careers, these men found it necessary to hide their sexual orientation.

The following chapter focuses on the role of professional athletes in society. Viewpoints in the chapter discuss athletes as role models, the role of the media in the perception of athletes, and whether athletes should become politicians.

> *"Pro athletes shouldn't be expected to be role models. But today's athletes need to understand that they are being viewed in a light that is much brighter than before."*

Professional Athletes Are Role Models

Richard Lowe

Richard Lowe is a journalist. In the following viewpoint, he contends that in a perfect world, parents—not athletes nor celebrities—would be role models to their children. However, Lowe argues that in the real world professional athletes are role models. Lowe points out that pro athletes need to understand the scrutiny on them and act as great role models for the kids who look up to them. These athletes must accept that it is part of the package when they become famous, Lowe concludes.

As you read, consider the following questions:

1. When did the infamous Charles Barkley Nike ad come out, according to the author?

2. In what year does Lowe report that the Michael Jordan Gatorade ad was first aired?

3. According to Lowe, what story about Tiger Woods became the top story on news stations in 2010?

[A] commercial by Nike featuring [professional basketball player] Charles Barkley came out in 1993. I was 7 years old when it was released, so I didn't participate in the debates that hatched from Barkley's words ["I am not a role model."]. But, in one sense, I agree with Barkley.

I don't think Barkley is a bad person. The fact is his life, and many other pro athletes' lives, should not be placed on a pedestal as the guide for telling people how to live. In a perfect world, all parents would be flawless and their children would see them as role models.

Not a Perfect World

But this is not a perfect world, and the reality is that kids figure out how they want to live their lives based on all aspects of their environment. Whether we like it or not, the celebrities in our world are prevalent in a youth's life. Whether they choose to be or not, celebrities are role models.

There used to be a time when the TV turned off at night. It wasn't because you hit the power button, but because the TV station stopped airing shows at a certain point in the night. A media boom took place in the 1980s and '90s that saw more sports, movies, and TV shows right at our fingertips. Twenty-four-hour stations really took off with channels like ESPN, MTV and CNN climbing up into their positions of dominating their respective genres.

Today's adults are unlike those of the past because we weren't amazed by the marvelous world of television. We grew up in a world that always had it. To see Barkley's commercial in '93 might have been seen as shocking to most families at the time, but for most kids it didn't register.

The Truth About Role Models

[It's] important not to put role models on a pedestal. If they're human and real then they need to be recognised as such. Everyone makes mistakes and so to follow anyone blindly is a mistake. Recognise that this is a 'guide' for you and not someone you have to follow exactly.

Mark Thomas, "The Importance of Role Models,"
HealthGuidance, 2012. www.healthguidance.org.

The Case of Michael Jordan

In 1991, Gatorade made a commercial that involved children singing a song wishing they could be like [professional basketball player] Michael Jordan, who was Gatorade's first athlete endorser. This type of marketing allowed Gatorade to continue its dominance in the world of sports drinks, while placing Michael Jordan in the spotlight. This commercial made Jordan a role model.

It's easy to idolize someone like Jordan when all you see from him is success. Now, obviously, as time has passed, Jordan has been revealed as, well, human. He cheated on his wife, got divorced and hasn't seen anything close to that same kind of success while he's been in charge of [professional basketball teams] the Washington Wizards and Charlotte Bobcats.

However, that doesn't stop the idolization of Jordan. Not even a bitter hall of fame induction speech put tarnish on the Jordan brand. He still sells his basketball shoes in record numbers. Players imitate his moves on the basketball court and his mannerisms off the court.

The media no longer look for the trendsetters of the past. They just want to know who is going to be the next Jordan.

Today's Pro Athletes

Today's professional athlete is happy to oblige with this request. Athletes are not only looking for the top dollar contract, but also the top dollar endorsement deals. They believe themselves to be an individual business as opposed to being an employee of an organization. It seems they want to be like Mike but have the attitude of Barkley. That's not to say Jordan didn't have the attitude. He just didn't put it out in the open for all the cameras to see.

Then again, maybe the opportunities weren't there for Jordan to be exposed like today's athlete. Everyone knew that Barkley was a tough competitor on the basketball court, but it wasn't until that Nike commercial that we knew about his views on being a role model. We view him differently because of it.

Tiger Woods provides a good contrast. He was idolized in golf but, after a car accident at his own home two years ago [2010], he is viewed differently. His extramarital affairs became the top story on stations where it shouldn't matter if Tiger Woods cheated on his wife. TMZ's sports section was built on the Tiger Woods story.

Athletes as Role Models

I've always been one who doesn't care about these athletes' personal lives. It's not my business. I wish them the best in everything in life, but I'm better off not knowing that Tiger Woods was cheating on his wife. Now everyone thinks he can't win a major tournament because of his emotional stability. It made us easily forget that he won his last major on one leg . . . literally!

Yes, parents need to raise their kids to not view celebrities as the holy grail, but there aren't many times when parents point at the TV and say, "You need to be just like [professional basketball players] Deron Williams or Jason Kidd." Kids tend to come up with that by themselves.

Pro athletes shouldn't be expected to be role models. But today's athletes need to understand that they are being viewed in a light that is much brighter than before. Actions speak louder now than before. Kids pay attention when an athlete shows up for community service events just as much as they pay attention to an athlete's performance in a game the night before.

Athletes, you may not want that kind of attention, but it comes with the package. You may not want to be a role model, but if you do wrong, you will be the example.

> "If sportswriters really wanted to do their readers a service, they would stop nagging the athletes to live up to children's expectations and start encouraging us fans to grow some scruples."

Professional Athletes Are Not Role Models

Raina Kelley

Raina Kelley is an associate editor at Newsweek. *In the following viewpoint, she argues that no adults consider athletes as role models because they know that they have been catered to from an early age and are often immature and irresponsible individuals. Kelley maintains that instead of nagging athletes to be better role models for children, sportswriters should be scrutinizing the role of sports fans in creating a climate in which the bad behavior of athletes is tolerated as a price of victory. Kelley contends that it is the fans who need to hold pro athletes responsible when their behavior is morally or ethically unacceptable.*

As you read, consider the following questions:

1. Why does Kelley believe that Nike loves Tiger Woods?

2. According to Kelley, how did fans react to the return of Michael Vick?

3. What media outlet is the only one examining the dark side of fandom, according to Kelley?

Ben Roethlisberger [a professional football player] is making controversial headlines again. So is [professional basketball player] Allen Iverson. The sports page has more scandal than *People* magazine. But so what? I have never in my life heard a grown-up say his role model was an athlete. I've heard people pick [philanthropist] Warren Buffett a bunch of times and [apartheid activist Nelson] Mandela, of course. When I ran with a more pretentious crowd, [musician] Bob Dylan and Holden Caulfield [the protagonist in J.D. Salinger's *The Catcher in the Rye*] were once offered up, but never [former professional football player] Joe Namath or [former professional basketball player] Magic Johnson. And you know why? Because any adult with a social IQ greater than a 10-year-old knows that athletes are hothouse flowers—worshiped, but isolated, from cradle to grave for their talent with a ball. In an interview with Nerve.com, Steven Ortiz, a sociology professor at Oregon State [University] and the author of several published studies on athletes' bad behavior, explained:

> "Spoiled-athlete syndrome begins early in sports socialization. From the time they could be picked out of a lineup because of their exceptional athletic ability, they've been pampered and catered to by coaches, classmates, teammates, family members and partners. As they get older, this becomes a pattern. Because they're spoiled, they feel they aren't accountable for their behaviors off the field. They're so used to people looking the other way."

But our sports-crazed society knew this long before Tiger [referring to professional golfer Tiger Woods] became a wolf. Despite all the adulation and money they get, few professional athletes get elected to political office and fewer still inspire national holidays or granite monuments. I love the Dallas Cowboys but I wouldn't let them date my friends. A fan's love is intense but ultimately self-serving—we love athletes who win. But we're not loony enough to give them any real power after they retire. Why then do so many columnists waste time complaining that athletes aren't good role models? Who's asking for that?

Facing the Truth About Athletes

Sure, kids look up to sports heroes but that's because children can't help but conflate an athlete's behavior on the field with all the hagiography [idolizing biography] their sponsors offer. When allegations of Woods's cheating first became public, CNN reported that "a golfing phenomenon almost from the cradle, he inspired countless young people with his multicultural background and effortless athleticism. Nike, one of his major sponsors, seized on the theme for a commercial in which children of various ages and races uttered the phrase 'I'm Tiger Woods.'" But only a child would believe that Nike loves Tiger for his multicultural background. Nike loves him because he wins.

If sportswriters really wanted to do their readers a service, they would stop nagging the athletes to live up to children's expectations and start encouraging us fans to grow some scruples. Because that's what the big sports sponsors like Nike understand about our love of athletes that the media doesn't—a good image is better than a bad one, but it's talent that sells sneakers. Of course there are exceptions, O.J. Simpson [a former professional football player who was tried but acquitted of murdering his ex-wife and her friend] being the most famous. But for the most part, fans will condone the criminal exploits of an athlete as long as he continues to perform on the field. As Stanley Teitelbaum, author of *Sports Heroes, Fallen Idols*, told *USA Today* in explaining why Tiger's reputation will heal, "We the fans have created that kind of climate. . . . It's what I call 'hero hunger.' It makes people feel better about themselves if they latch onto a hero who does well." Which means we don't really care when athletes screw up—unless that is, they screw up with the ball in their hands. Remember when all the pundits said fans would never accept Michael Vick back into the NFL [National Football League] after he served time in prison for running a dogfighting ring? They did. I suspect Tiger will be greeted with open arms (platonic, of course) upon his return to golf despite the World Wide Web's consensus that he's a cheating, lying creep with questionable taste in women. Indeed, stories bemoaning his absence (for the good of the game) are already popping up.

The Pitfalls of Moral Relativism

This is the kind of thing sportswriters should be chastising us for—I want to be told there wouldn't be so many convicted felons in the NFL if the fans didn't write off all their bad behavior as a cost of winning. We know we're captive to a group of prima donnas who know they can get away with almost murder just because they can hit a 90-mph fastball out of the park. Not even die-hard groupies confuse an athlete's statistics with the content of his character, but you need to remind us from time to time that such moral relativism isn't a good thing. Please, I'd forgive [quarterback for the Dallas Cowboys] Tony Romo for mugging my mother if the Cowboys won the Super Bowl, but that doesn't make it right. What if one day we become unable to tell the difference between cosseting divas and suborning felons? And if Ben Roethlisberger has done even 20 percent of what he's been accused of doing, that day has already come.

Sports journalists should make it their mission to show sports fans our part in all this. The average nonfan is appalled by the alleged exploits of athletes like Ben Roethlisberger or Tiger Woods. But aside from [sportscaster] Bryant Gumbel and his team over at HBO Sports, you don't hear much from

ESPN or *Sports Illustrated* about the dark side of this national obsession. More of them need to do just as Christopher Hitchens did here at *Newsweek* when he wrote, in a piece about the Olympics, "Whether it's the exacerbation of national rivalries that you want—as in Africa this year—or the exhibition of the most depressing traits of the human personality (guns in locker rooms, golf clubs wielded in the home, dogs maimed and tortured at stars' homes to make them fight, dope and steroids everywhere), you need only look to the wide world of sports for the most rank and vivid examples." So if we really want to create role models for our kids, why not start with ourselves? Because only children confuse sports stars with humanitarians; the rest of us know better.

Professional Athletes Are Drawn to Politics

J. Patrick Dobel

J. Patrick Dobel is an educator and blogger. In the following viewpoint, he perceives athletes to be natural politicians because they are highly competitive, are already adept at handling the press, have a high name recognition, and can trade on their good reputation to get votes. Because most politics are local, he explains, professional athletes can get elected in areas in which they played and have an advantage over other candidates. It is interesting, Dobel adds, that most pro football players run as Republicans, while pro basketball players become Democratic politicians. Dobel posits that these political divisions may coordinate with the characteristics of these sports such as individualism and teamwork.

As you read, consider the following questions:

1. How many terms does the author say that Steve Largent served in the US Congress?

J. Patrick Dobel, "Athlete Politicians: Basketball Democrats & Football Republicans," Point of the Game, March 15, 2012. www.pointofthegame.blogspot.com. Copyright © 2012 by J. Patrick Dobel. All rights reserved. Reproduced by permission.

2. According to the author, how many terms did Bill Bradley serve in the US Senate?

3. What percentage of the NBA is made up of black players, according to Dobel?

Name recognition alchemizes electoral politics, and name recognition with high positives generates electoral gold. This link makes athletics and electoral politics natural fits, and more than a few successful athletes have parlayed their positive fame into electoral victories. Using a totally nonscientific sample of largely ex-professional players, I think that the two sports—football and basketball—launch very different political types.

The Connection Between Politics and Sports

Let's start with the similarities of electoral politics and sports. All elite athletes are fierce competitors dedicated to winning. Elite athletes stay in shape and are incredibly driven and persistent; they don't give up and learn to handle failure and adapt. In modern sports, they learn to handle negative press and personal attacks as well as revel in success. They know how fickle the public can be but hold their professional focus. These character traits prepare them well for electoral politics.

Finally most athletes earn their fame in a local area, and electoral politics remains resolutely local despite the best efforts of rational PACs [political action committees]. Most of the politicians I cite either returned home like [Steve] Largent, [J.C.] Watts or [Kevin] Johnson or built their political base where they played long term like [Jack] Kemp, [Bill] Bradley or [Dave] Bing. They enter at strong local positions such as mayor or US House seats.

So let's think about the hypothetical relations between politics and football and basketball.

Offhand a couple football names come to mind. Steve Largent, the great receiver for the Seattle Seahawks, returned home to Oklahoma and entered politics as a conservative Republican. He served four terms in the US House of Representatives but lost in his bid to become Republican governor. J.C. Watts returned home to Oklahoma and ran successfully for the US House of Representatives as a black conservative Republican. [Philadelphia] Eagles guard Jon Runyan presently serves in the US House from New Jersey as a conservative. Republican Jack Kemp, one of the most dynamic and interesting politicians of the late twentieth century, was elected from his base as the Buffalo Bills quarterback. He served 18 years in the House and later as the secretary of HUD [Housing and Urban Development] under George H. Bush as well as a vice presidential candidate. Non pro but very, very football, Tom Osborne, the longtime football coach at Nebraska, served four terms in the US House and lost his bid to win the governorship.

Football and the Republican Party

Why would football players make good conservative Republicans? Good question and I will right away eliminate all the head injuries as some wags have suggested. First, elite athletes believe in individual self-discipline and personal responsibility. The vast majority of players come from working-class or deeply disadvantaged backgrounds. All of them achieved success as self-made men and will not believe in an entitled or "handout" based world. Second, football depends upon strong authority. Players thrive under strong authoritative leadership. The authority combines with ordered cooperation and teamwork. Third, teams are voluntary associations where people earn their spots in a brutal and relentless meritocracy. Successful teams align voluntary self-disciplined effort and skills with an absolute commitment to common authority—one mind, one team, one effort, one leader. Finally, violence and

Some Former Athletes Who Became Politicians

Dave Bing—former NBA player and current mayor of Detroit (2009–present)

Bill Bradley—former NBA player and former US congressman from New Jersey (1979–1997)

Kevin Johnson—former NBA player and current mayor of Sacramento (2008–present)

Jack Kemp—former NFL player and former US congressman from New York (1971–1989)

Steve Largent—former NFL player and former US congressman from Oklahoma (1994–2002)

Jon Runyan—former NFL player and current US congressman from New Jersey (2011–present)

Arnold Schwarzenegger—former World Amateur Bodybuilding Champion and former governor of California (2003–2011)

Compiled by editors, 2012.

aggressiveness dominate the world of football. Teams win with brains but ultimately with the consistent, skillful and borderline legal applications of force and coercion. Football is not just about competition and zero-sum win or lose situations but about a world saturated with aggression and violence.

Modern Republicanism, at least, fits naturally with a worldview of being surrounded by violent enemies and depending upon a radical self-made effort where people owe little to each other, unless they do so in a voluntary association. It also coexists uneasily with a world of strong authoritarian leadership to mobilize people in a threatening and aggressive world.

Basketball and the Democratic Party

Basketball has a long tradition of Democrats. Mo Udall, long-time Arizona congressman and presidential candidate, played basketball for the Denver Nuggets. Bill Bradley played for years with the New York Knicks and ended up serving three terms in the US Senate representing New Jersey as well as being strongly considered for the presidency. Tom McMillen played basketball at Maryland and professional at Washington. He later served three terms as a member of the US House in Maryland before losing his seat in a redistricting battle.

One of the issues that lead me to thinking about this was watching Kevin Johnson, the mayor of Sacramento, lead negotiations to keep the Sacramento Kings at his birth city. He started economic development companies in his hometown after going back for his degree at [the University of] California[, Berkeley] and then getting a divinity degree at Harvard. Dave Bing was elected as a strong reform-minded mayor in Detroit after playing for the Pistons for 16 years and then founding a successful local business.

Now why might basketball turn out Democrats? Well race might seem obvious, since 82 percent of NBA [National Basketball Association] players are black compared to 65% in football, except football culture trumps race in the case of folks like J.C. Watts or Lynn Swann. Elite basketball athletes would share the same mind-set of self-made individuals as well as the disciplined and focus competitive worldview. But basketball presents a very different view of authority and how the world works. Basketball unfolds as a continuous sport, not a reset sport. No one gets to stop after each event and call plays and start over. Authority is not authoritarian in such conditions. It must be adaptable, fluid and open to a wider range of permutations in real time. In basketball you don't just do what you are told, you see and adapt while the coach watches from the side. While physical, basketball does not possess nearly the level of sheer violence or injury. It requires aggressiveness but of a much more blended type. Basketball never stops moving. It is chaotic and fast and requires incessant and fluid awareness to master the sport. Players relate to authority differently.

Authority and Teamwork

Authority remains more fluid since coaches cannot stop play each play and impose order. The power of the floor general or point guard grows and takes far more time. The teamwork is much less rigid. More room exists for egos and individuality because the teams are smaller and more exposed rather than the faceless weaponized modern football players. Basketball presents a world with much more individualized play, more styles, more chaos and much less overt and direct aggressive violence. It also requires a comfort with endless, vaguely ordered chaos.

If you watch the modern Democratic politics, it remains a more chaotic, pluralistic and diffuse coalition. The politics require adaptability and movement and comfort with chaos and innovation; authority is simply far less certain and diversity of style far wider. The worldview opens to more than just zero-sum solutions or aggressive and violent enemies.

I may think more about this and wonder what to do with [former governor of California] Arnold Schwarzenegger and bodybuilding or [former governor of Minnesota] Jesse Ventura and professional wrestling, but that is another story, as is baseball.

As I think more about football and Republicans I remember that Richard Nixon played football at Whittier College, Dwight Eisenhower played football at West Point until he was injured. Gerald Ford played football at Michigan and Ronald Reagan played football at Notre Dame. No wait! He played George ["The] Gipper" [Gipp] in the movie *Knute Rockne[, All American]*, but in modern America there is no difference.

> "Keep in mind that the sports-industrial complex tends to produce narrow-minded, self-centered, ethically challenged mercenaries who are deeply submissive to established authority while being fiercely dedicated to winning by any means possible."

Professional Athletes Should Not Become Politicians

Robert Lipsyte

Robert Lipsyte is an author and sports journalist. In the following viewpoint, he states that professional athletes should not become politicians because the very traits that made them good players—fierce competitiveness, self-obsession, and submission to authority—are the very things that make them bad politicians. Professional athletes, Lipsyte maintains, can also be ignorant, spoiled, and narcissistic, more errant qualities for a politician. In fact, he concludes, by looking at the roster of recent pro athletes who turned politicians, it can be seen that the majority of them have been major disappointments.

As you read, consider the following questions:

1. Who does Lipsyte consider to be a rare exception to the No-Jock mandate?

Robert Lipsyte, "Leave 'Em in the Locker Room," TomDispatch.com, October 19, 2010.

2. Which of Chris Dudley's political positions does the author regard as problematic?

3. How many pro wrestlers died at a young age in 2010, according to Lipsyte?

Old sportswriters are always being asked for tips on big games. Here's one for the biggest game on the schedule: Never vote for a jock.

This is particularly good advice in a political season whose starting lineup includes Chris Dudley, a former NBA [National Basketball Association] backup center running for governor of Oregon; Linda McMahon, cofounder of World Wrestling Entertainment running for senator from Connecticut; and Heath Shuler, a former NFL [National Football League] quarterback, scrambling for a third term as a member of the House from North Carolina. They are already campaigning to fit into the woeful tradition of Jim Bunning, Jesse Ventura, Tom Osborne, and [Wilmer] Vinegar Bend Mizell, athletic role models whose narcissism, ignorance, and conservatism helped them make a seamless transition from entertaining people to exploiting them.

Keep in mind that the sports-industrial complex tends to produce narrow-minded, self-centered, ethically challenged mercenaries who are deeply submissive to established authority while being fiercely dedicated to winning by any means possible. Or as one of my old political advisors, Sam Hall Kaplan, a former *New York Times* and *Los Angeles Times* reporter, puts it: "A pol who learned as an athlete just who ultimately butters his bread can be counted on to continue to wave to the crowds while doing the bidding of the owners." And the owners these days, thanks to the umpires (. . . er, Supreme Court) are likely to be unnamed billionaire warlords donating to right-wing candidates through dummy organizations that have no requirement to open their books to the voters.

The Exception to the Rule

Let's get this year's [2010's] rare exception to my No-Jock mandate out of the way right now. Alan Page, running again for associate justice of the Minnesota Supreme Court, is that rare all-star on the field and on the high bench.

As Jay Weiner, author of *This Is Not Florida: How Al Franken Won the Minnesota Senate Recount*, reminds us: "One of the wisest and most pointed legal opinions to come out of the recount" of that embattled 2008 election was written by "a picture of Black Robed Dignity" who had once been a "Purple People Eater." Defensive tackle Page had a 15-season National Football League Hall of Fame career, mostly with the Minnesota Vikings on that fearsome purple-uniformed defensive line.

Two other Democrats, both out of office now, once earned my own grateful votes—New York governor Mario Cuomo (minor league baseball) and Senator Bill Bradley (two championships with the New York Knicks).

But after that, a team of losers.

Mostly Republican, Mostly Busts

Leading off our sorry starting lineup for 2012 is Heath Shuler, a Blue Dog Democrat and real estate investor. He was also a former Washington Redskins and New Orleans Saints quarterback, rated by ESPN in 2004 as the fourth-biggest NFL draft bust of all time and the 17th biggest "sports flop" of the past 25 years. Of course, those are not good enough reasons to vote against him (unless you happened to root for one of his teams).

But here's a good reason: His vote against the Patient Protection and Affordable Care Act because health care reform could be detrimental to the economy. He was for what he termed "common-sense incremental change" which, in reality, meant slowing the game down until time runs out.

Of further concern is Shuler's membership in "the Family," that creepy D.C. frat of evangelical Christian right-wingers like Senators Tom Coburn and Jim DeMint, and Congressmen Zach Wamp and Bart Stupak, and such hypocritical God-Squadders as John Ensign, Chip Pickering, and Mark Sanford. Shuler has bunked down in their infamous locker room, the so-called "C Street house." Jeff Sharlet, author of *C Street: The Fundamentalist Threat to American Democracy*, writes about the Family's "explicit dedication to the ruling class" in America and abroad, and also links the group to Uganda's murderous anti-homosexuality bill.

A Weak Roster

Shuler may be an even worse politician than he was a pro athlete. His predecessors in the Jock House, all Republicans, were certainly a mixed bag. Jack Kemp, an MVP [most valuable player] quarterback in the old American Football League, who twice led the Buffalo Bills to the championship, served nine terms. A basically decent and intelligent man, [George] Bush the First's secretary of Housing and Urban Development, and Bob Dole's vice-presidential running mate, Kemp was a [Ronald] Reagan supply-sider whose major piece of legislation, the Kemp-Roth Tax Cut [officially the Economic Recovery Tax Act of 1981], helped put the trickle in trickle-down economics while the guys up top enjoyed the waterfall.

After Kemp, the roster only grows weaker with Wilmer (Vinegar Bend) Mizell, a left-hander in his nine-year major league pitching career and a right-winger in three terms from North Carolina; Jim Ryun, one of the world's greatest milers and one of the most conservative Kansans to reach the congressional Oz since Toto ran the Yellow Brick Road; and Tom Osborne, a former NFL wide receiver who, before scoring his House seat, coached Nebraska for 25 years, famously with stars who should have been in jail. (He once asked me, "Would you rather they were on my team or in your neighborhood?")

As a three-term representative, he received a lifetime rating of 83 from the American Conservative Union.

The Big Boys

Back to the jock-pol lowlights of 2012: Chris Dudley was a strong rebounder and shot blocker for several teams over 16 seasons, a tribute to his athleticism, but he was also the NBA's all-time second-worst foul shooter (the mark of a weak work ethic), setting the league record for 13 missed free throws in a row. This is not a good enough reason to vote against him for governor of Oregon.

And the jury (actually it's an IRS [Internal Revenue Service] matter at the moment) is out on the $350,000 tax deduction he took for allowing a local fire department to burn down a 4,500-square-foot house on his property. He later built an 8,500-square-foot home on that scorched earth plot and so ignited a campaign controversy: Was it legal or just another example of an entitled jock bending the rules?

Still, no blatant foul. Yet.

On the other hand, his positions on the environment and the minimum wage put him out of bounds—or rather, when it comes to the environment, his studiously ominous lack of a position. Throughout his campaign he has dodged questions about natural resources and global warming ("Global warming exists. And mankind contributes. How much? I don't know. . . .") for a good reason: timber and agricultural interests are his major financial backers. According to Jeff Mapes in the *Oregonian*, "Jon Isaacs of the Oregon League of Conservation Voters . . . noted that in addition to supporting higher logging levels, Dudley has said he is against a permanent ban on oil drilling off the Oregon coast and opposes Ballot Measure 76, which would continue the 15% diversion from lottery profits for parks and wildlife habitat."

Like most jocks, Dudley is not sensitive to the people in the grandstands. He can say (or joke?) that he understands "minority" concerns, having been a white man in the predominately black NBA, and he can say, "It doesn't make sense that our waitresses are getting tips plus the highest minimum wage in the country." Not exactly slam dunks, either of them.

Schwarzenegger and Ventura

At 6 feet 11 inches tall, Dudley's height puts him in the same league with at least two oversized jock-governors, Arnold Schwarzenegger and Jesse Ventura, who initially rose through the ranks of sports, and may yet encourage Charles Barkley to run for governor of Alabama in 2014 as he has promised/threatened for years. Currently a sportscaster, Barkley is an NBA Hall of Famer and, more important for a politician, a member of the media's all-interview team. He's best known for a Nike ad in which he said, "I am not a role model."

[Sam] Hall Kaplan, who covered Schwarzenegger's first gubernatorial campaign for a local Los Angeles TV station, sums up the Gubernator's California years this way: "The jock's need to dominate and to win at any costs certainly applies to his term of office. He has shown little initiative and little imagination, while playing to the crowds and the cronies. Particularly onerous has been the deep cuts in public education while declining to face up to the need for progressive tax reform."

Weiner, who had a close-up view of Ventura while working as a reporter at the *Minneapolis Star Tribune*, summed up the former Minnesota governor, Dudley's other potential role model, this way: He "could not separate the faux professional wrestling world from the real political and public policy world. To him, all the world was a stage and not the hard work of compromise. You just don't strike deals with Hulk Hogan, ya know. You win or you lose, or you jump off the ropes and cause a stir. Or, as Ventura did, you leave the political arena because you're not the center of attention anymore."

Savvy Businesswoman

Ventura may be gone from politics—he hosts a TV show about conspiracy theories—but wrestling is still trying to get a hold on us.

Linda McMahon is campaigning for the Senate in Connecticut as a savvy businesswoman who will bring fiscal restraint to a strapped, overblown state government through the usual Reaganomic supply-side measures, including—of course—various corporate tax cuts and the abolition of the estate tax and the gift tax. She may end up spending $50 million of her own money to join the senatorial ranks. No big deal. She and husband Vince built World Wrestling Entertainment [WWE] into a billion-dollar global enterprise, proving she can grow things, and to prove she knows how to enjoy her money, there is the McMahons' 47-foot yacht, *Sexy Bitch*.

Probably even more than pro football players—those other violent wide-bodies—wrestlers need steroids and pain medication to stay big, play hurt, and maintain their relentless schedule. (Many wrestlers, including Hulk Hogan, have admitted to steroid use.) One result may be that professional wrestlers are 20 times more likely than professional football players to die before the age of 45, according to a *USA Today* investigation.

Four wrestlers have died this year [2010] including, most recently, 29-year-old Lance McNaught (who fought as Lance Cade). His death of heart failure, after steroid and pain-pill abuse to keep himself in the game, brought up the issue of McMahon's culpability. How much did she know about her workers' drug use? Were her employees under so much pressure to perform—or lose their jobs—that the corporation should be blamed for their deaths? WWE conveniently deals with its wrestlers as independent contractors, offering no benefits, not even health insurance.

The Drama of the WWE

McMahon has successfully deflected confrontational campaign trail questions about McNaught's steroid use and the trail of dead wrestlers strewn behind the WWE. While she sometimes claims to know little about what she likes to call the "creative" side of wrestling—after all, she's the serious businesswoman— she has actually performed in the ring.

If you think wrestling is merely slabs of beef colliding in orchestrated mayhem, you haven't been paying attention. Big events include scripted mini-dramas that can play on for months among wrestlers, male and female, and even have included the McMahons. In one ongoing soap opera, Linda is being "emotionally abused" by Vince and falls into a "coma." When she awakes (in the ring), she accuses him of philandering and pretends to kick him in the groin.

You want that in the statehouse? We don't even need to go into whether or not she wants to decrease the minimum wage—as she once implied but now has backtracked on. My suspicion is that, if elected, she could well compete with the departing Republican senator from Kentucky Jim Bunning for worst jock-senator in history.

Last Pitch

As you might know, it was as a Philadelphia Phillies pitcher that Bunning tossed a perfect game against the New York Mets in 1964. It was the high point of a 17-year Hall of Fame career. It also gave both sports and political writers license to hurl the word "imperfect" at his two-term senatorial record. In 2006, *Time* called him one of the worst five senators of his time. *Time* dubbed him "the underperformer." In their 2007 conservative/liberal rankings, *National Journal* had Bunning as the second most conservative senator, trailing only that "Family" man Jim DeMint of South Carolina.

In his final innings, Bunning notoriously prevented the Senate from extending unemployment benefits for more than

1.2 million workers for more than a month. When fellow senators begged him to halt his filibuster, according to Politico, Bunning's reply was: "Tough shit." Describing Bunning as "loutish, eccentric, and mean," Joe Conason on Salon.com accused him of using the Jim Bunning Foundation to shelter his fees from the baseball memorabilia shows at which he appeared to sell autographs.

It was the Republican Party that sent Bunning to the showers a couple of months ago. He decided not to run again because of lack of GOP support and funds. Score a rare one for the GOP. Bunning was my quintessential incumbent jerk-jock politician who you should never vote for. And he was stupid. Case in point: He said, "I watch Fox News to get my information."

Periodical and Internet Sources Bibliography

The following articles have been selected to supplement the diverse views presented in this chapter.

| Eric Anderson | "For Gay Athletes, a Harsh Spotlight," *New York Times*, July 2, 2012. |

Ben Austen   "The Pro Athletes Are Invading Politics," *Wall Street Journal*, November 2, 2010.

Buzz Bissinger   "Major League Homophobia Isn't Going Away," *The Daily Beast*, May 4, 2011.

Frank Bruni   "The Barriers to Openness," *New York Times*, September 22, 2012.

Ian Carey   "When Will We See Openly Gay Players in the MLB, NFL, NBA and NHL?," *Huffington Post*, September 26, 2012.

Aimee Frise   "Professional Athletes: True Role Models?," *Sonoma State Star*, December 5, 2009.

Brandon Land   "Professional Athletes as Role Models: Is It Their Job?," *Bleacher Report*, April 9, 2010. http://bleacherreport.com.

Robert Lipsyte   "Sports, Politics Don't Often Mix," *USA Today*, May 28, 2012.

Bob Mand   "Simmonds' Slur Incident Indicative of Hockey's Deeper Struggle," TheHockeyWriters .com, September 28, 2011.

Isabella Moschen   "A Timeline of Incremental Progress," *New York Times*, September 22, 2012.

Chris Pope   "Embracing Gay Athletes in Professional Sports," TheGoodPoint.com, February 5, 2011.

OPPOSING
VIEWPOINTS®
SERIES

CHAPTER 2

How Should Pro Sports Treat Performance-Enhancing Drugs and Injuries?

Chapter Preface

On February 17, 2011, a fifty-year-old man named Dave Duerson was found dead at his Florida home from a self-inflicted gunshot wound. A retired professional football player, Duerson was regarded as one of the best players at his position during his career with the National Football League (NFL), earning four trips to the Pro Bowl, the league's annual all-star game. He was also a member of two world championship teams, earning Super Bowl rings with the 1986 Chicago Bears and the 1990 New York Giants. In 1987 Duerson was the recipient of the NFL Man of the Year Award. All in all, Duerson had an accomplished career.

However, Duerson's post-football life was troubled. In the years after his 1993 retirement, he flourished: He built a successful meat business, became active in the NFL Players Association, and was invited to join the board of trustees of his alma mater, the University of Notre Dame. However, around 2005 the crippling effects of chronic traumatic encephalopathy (CTE), a progressive degenerative disease that is caused by repeated head injuries, began to appear. He began to make bad business decisions, including missing payments and deadlines. There were reports of domestic violence in his marriage. He fought with vendors and creditors. By 2008 both his business and marriage were failing.

It seems evident that Duerson's football experience, and his three documented concussions, had left him with CTE, a disease with symptoms including dementia, headaches, tremors, confusion, aggression, and depression. Professional athletes frequently suffer from CTE because of the repeated blows to the head they take during practice and games.

In the months before his death, Duerson realized that something was seriously wrong; right before his suicide, he told his family that there was a problem with his brain. He then shot himself in the chest, leaving his brain intact. He left a message that he wanted researchers to find out what was wrong. Researchers at Boston University's Center for the Study of Traumatic Encephalopathy performed an extensive brain autopsy that confirmed Duerson's instinct: He had been suffering with advanced brain damage, caused by the progressive disease CTE.

Duerson's tragic suicide was one of a series of suicides of former NFL players, some of whom were also thought to suffer from CTE. On May 2, 2012, the sporting world was shocked to learn of the suicide of Junior Seau, a ten-time All-Pro and twelve-time Pro Bowl selection who had played linebacker for the San Diego Chargers, Miami Dolphins, and New England Patriots. Retired from the NFL since 2010, Seau had suffered from chronic insomnia that was thought might have stemmed from repeated head injuries that he received playing football, although there was no recorded evidence of a history of concussions.

Like Duerson, Seau shot himself in the chest; many commentators believe he did that to allow his brain to be studied. The researchers at Boston University's Center for the Study of Traumatic Encephalopathy also performed the autopsy for Seau and concluded that there was no sign of the extensive brain damage that Duerson had. However, further testing of Seau's brain was done at the National Institute of Neurological Disorders and Stroke at the National Institutes of Health (NIH). The results of those tests have not been released by the family.

A number of former players have filed lawsuits against the NFL over its handling of concussions, charging that the league had failed to address the link between concussions and CTE. High-profile suicides of former players, such as Duerson and Seau, have brought media attention to the subject of head injuries in sports. It has also illuminated the way sports leagues approach the problem of concussions, which is one of the subjects explored in the following chapter focusing on the treatment of performance-enhancing drugs and injuries in professional sports. Other viewpoints in the chapter examine the issues of athlete suicide and steroid use.

| "Rather than being banned . . . steroids should be available, under a doctor's supervision, to any pro or amateur adult athlete who wants them."

Professional Athletes Should Be Allowed to Use Steroids

Charles Leroux

Charles Leroux is a senior correspondent for the Chicago Tribune. *In the following viewpoint, he reports on the controversial views of Norman Fost, a renowned physician and medical ethicist who believes that athletes should be able to use steroids under a doctor's supervision. According to Fost, the movement to ban anabolic steroids in sports is antidrug hysteria and not based on medical fact. Steroids are not unnatural, do not undermine the integrity of the sport, and are safe if supervised closely by a trained doctor, Fost insists. Plus, as Fost concludes and Leroux explains, it is hypocritical to single out steroids when athletes use all sorts of performance-enhancing techniques, substances, equipment, and training methods.*

As you read, consider the following questions:

1. In what Olympics was the American swimmer Rick Du-Mont stripped of a gold medal for taking a banned substance, according to the author?

2. According to a study cited by the author, what chance does a football player spending more than three years in the NFL have to suffer a permanent disability?

3. According to tests cited by the viewpoint, what percentage of athletes were using steroids in 2003?

How can the accomplishments of [Barry] Bonds, [Mark] McGwire, [Sammy] Sosa and others of the "steroid era" of baseball be compared to those of [Hank] Aaron or [Babe] Ruth? Can Major League Baseball and the National Football League and the others ever get drugs out of their systems? Will the athletes named as users in the Mitchell Report [referring to a report prepared by Senator George J. Mitchell after a twenty-one-month investigation into the use of anabolic steroids and human growth hormone in Major League Baseball] face futures threatened by cancer, heart attack, stroke? What will come of the House committee hearings, now postponed until February [2008]? Is there any tarnish remover strong enough to put the shine back on sports in America?

Norman Fost

As the controversy over use of anabolic steroids by athletes swirls like a wind-whipped snowstorm, Norman Fost, professor of pediatric medicine and director of the program in bioethics at the University of Wisconsin, is a center of calm and certainty. He says, as he has for many years and virtually alone, that the maelstrom is nothing more than "the hypocrisy, bad facts, inconsistency and moral incoherence of anti-drug hysteria."

To him, athletes who take banned performance-enhancing drugs are as morally and ethically blameless as the pole vaulters who quickly converted from bamboo poles to fiberglass when they saw a competitive edge. Rather than being banned, he insists, steroids should be available, under a doctor's supervision, to any pro or amateur adult athlete who wants them.

For his contrarian stance, the soft-spoken, 68-year-old tennis- and basketball-playing sports junkie who will, he said, "watch anything that moves," has been roundly vilified. . . .

A Stellar Resume

If Fost is a wacko, he likely has the most stellar resume in the wacko world. His bachelor's degree is from Princeton, his M.D. from Yale. His residency was at Johns Hopkins and his master's in public health came from Harvard. At Wisconsin in 1973, he founded one of the earliest and most highly regarded and copied bioethics programs in the nation.

"Norm has always been provocative and controversial," said Dr. Mark Siegler, director of MacLean Center for Clinical Medical Ethics at the University of Chicago and a friend and colleague of Fost's since the '70s. "But his views are always presented in a careful, thoughtful way, and come from a depth of insight and clear thinking."

New Jersey–born Fost recalled that his father, also a pediatrician, was "skeptical when it came to conventional wisdom. He was smart, funny and a pit bull about honesty."

Those genes kicked in vis-à-vis sports for Fost when, in the 1972 Munich Summer Olympics, an American swimmer, Rick DuMont, was stripped of a gold medal for taking a banned substance, ephedrine. It was contained in an over-the-counter cold medicine that he took, with the permission of his team doctor, to relieve asthma symptoms.

"Superficial Reporting"

"I started thinking about the line between treatment and enhancement," recalled Fost, who takes even aspirin reluctantly.

"As time went by, I kept reading more and more superficial reporting about how taking enhancing drugs was immoral."

In 1983, he wrote an editorial for the *New York Times* titled "Let 'em Take Steroids," an attack on the growing body of conventional and, he thought, bogus wisdom.

At the 1988 Seoul Olympics, Canadian sprinter Ben Johnson would leave in disgrace, portrayed as, Fost said, "a combination of Charles Manson and Adolf Hitler. But the American swimmer Janet Evans was hailed as representing everything good and great."

The difference was that Johnson tested positive for the use of an anabolic steroid while Evans, after her 5,000-meter gold medal win, was lauded for keeping secret from other teams the newly developed, high-tech fabric swimsuit she said helped her to victory.

Watching this morality play of good and evil on his TV, Fost wondered, "Why was Johnson condemned for taking a performance-enhancing drug while Evans' use of a performance-enhancing suit was praised?"

Fost then wrote another *New York Times* op-ed piece, this one titled "Ben Johnson: The World's Fastest Scapegoat."

More Hypocrisy

Just as he found hypocrisy in the stance that one form of enhancement is immoral while another is OK, he found it as well in the hue and cry concerning the health horrors associated with steroid use. He read medical journals from around the world and found no deaths tied to anabolic steroid use, no side effects for adults beyond acne, hair loss, infertility, lowered voices in women—mostly cosmetic and reversible effects. He allows that, during use, bad lipids in the blood rise while the good decline but said: "This gets translated by the press into statements that there is an increased incidence of heart disease or stroke. I don't know of any evidence of that."

As to so-called "roid rage," out-of-control anger associated with steroid use, he says there are statistically so few cases that conclusions about cause and effect are hard to make. Fost is more interested in controlling the behavior than the steroids. "If people are worried about physical or sexual assault by athletes on steroids, they should be equally worried about them by athletes who are not on steroids."

Charles Yesalis, a steroids expert and epidemiologist at Pennsylvania State University, has expressed doubts about "roid rage" as well and has been quoted in media reports as saying, "You take a state college on any given weekend and you will see as many cases of alcohol-induced rage as you will see in a hundred years with anabolic steroids."

Recent Research Findings

Last February's issue of *Behavioral Neuroscience* reported on research conducted at Northeastern University by a group headed by Richard Melloni Jr., associate professor of psychology. The group injected a cocktail of various steroids into adolescent hamsters and found the animals becoming aggressive and remaining that way weeks after their last injection.

"After tearing apart thousands upon thousands of animal brains," Melloni said in a telephone interview, "I've concluded that these [anabolic steroids] are dangerous substances and should continue to be banned. They produce dramatic effects on developing systems in adolescents and on already developed systems. Some of the effects seem to reverse when the steroids are no longer used. Some don't."

Melloni's is one of the few labs doing such research and has looked only at animals, though he says research on human brains may become possible with improved neuroimaging technology.

Fost absolutely opposes giving steroids to adolescents because steroid use can stunt growth. He urges stringent testing of young athletes, and, for those distributing steroids to children: "Hanging followed by a fair trial."

Drug Hysteria

In all the health and morality questions about steroids, Fost said: "It's as though the drug hysteria serves as a distraction from more serious issues. You'd be hard-pressed to find a single death associated with steroid use, yet the TV cameras keep showing [Red Sox manager] Terry Francona drooling disgusting spit from something [chewing tobacco] that has a very high cancer rate associated with it.

"You have 400,000 deaths a year due to tobacco and tens of thousands of alcohol-related deaths, a substance heavily promoted by Major League Baseball, yet the president and Congress and the press have virtually nothing to say about tobacco and alcohol in athletics, but lots to say about steroids. A football player spending more than three years in the NFL has an 80 to 90 percent chance, according to one study, of some permanent disability, but the NFL produces films focusing on the most vicious hits. The dangers to health in sports today come not from enhancement but the sport itself."

Is the Tide Turning?

The governing bodies of national and international sports and groups such as the [World] Anti-Doping Agency still hold firm in banning steroids. The federal government continues to sponsor public service announcements warning of the dangers associated with use. But lately, some scientists, lawyers and writers have come around to Fost's stance.

"I'm not so much the loneliest guy anymore," Fost said.

Nonetheless, he has no illusions that the boogeyman will go away any time soon. He likens the persistent myths on steroids to those concerning the Iraq weapons of mass destruction.

"Even when it came out that there were no such weapons," he said, "having heard over and over that they existed, 40 percent of the public still believed it."

Counterpoints to
Some Common Arguments

Dr. Norman Fost has ticked through his arguments against the objections to steroid use often enough that he can do it by rote, stopping only when his listener says something that indicates he gets Fost's point. Then he stops, smiles, points an index finger and says, "Bingo."

Steroids give an unfair advantage. "There are a lot of things in sports that are unfair. In some football games, my beloved [University of Wisconsin] Badgers' offensive line may outweigh opponents by 60 pounds. That's unfair. It is hypocritical for leaders in Major League Baseball to trumpet their concern about fair competition when one team [the Yankees] is allowed to have a payroll three times larger than most of its competitors.

"Steroids are unfair only if there's unequal access. Removing the ban would give equal access. Also, as long as they are banned, steroids will come from people making them in their bathtubs, no clinical trials as to safety, no oversight of manufacturing process, no long-term studies. If steroids are harmful over the long term, that would be good to know, but under the current conditions, we may never find out."

Athletes are coerced into using steroids. "That would mean there's the use of force or a threat of deprivation. Steroids are an offer to be better off than you are, just as signing up with a professional team is an opportunity to be better off than you are. In the first year of testing in 2003, with the results anonymous and with no penalties, about 6 percent were found to be using steroids but 94 percent were not. If there was coercion, it wasn't working."

What Are Steroids?

"Anabolic steroids" is the familiar name for synthetic variants of the male sex hormone testosterone. The proper term for these compounds is *anabolic-androgenic steroids* (abbreviated AAS)—"anabolic" referring to muscle building and "androgenic" referring to increased male sexual characteristics.

Anabolic steroids can be legally prescribed to treat conditions resulting from steroid hormone deficiency, such as delayed puberty, as well as diseases that result in loss of lean muscle mass, such as cancer and AIDS. But some athletes, bodybuilders, and others abuse these drugs in an attempt to enhance performance and/or improve their physical appearance.

Anabolic steroids are usually either taken orally or injected into the muscles, although some are applied to the skin as a cream or gel. Doses taken by abusers may be 10 to 100 times higher than doses prescribed to treat medical conditions.

Steroids are typically taken intermittently rather than continuously, both to avert unwanted side effects and to give the body's hormonal system a periodic chance to recuperate. Continuous use of steroids can decrease the body's responsiveness to the drugs (tolerance) as well as cause the body to stop producing its own testosterone; breaks in steroid use are believed to redress these issues. . . .

In addition, users often combine several different types of steroids and/or incorporate other steroidal or nonsteroidal supplements in an attempt to maximize their effectiveness, a practice referred to as "stacking."

"Drug Facts: Anabolic Steroids,"
National Institute on Drug Abuse, July 2012.

Steroids are unnatural. "Testosterone is made by the body. It's the most natural of all steroids. The rest are synthetic. Yet testosterone is the one steroid that we know does cause cancer and therefore is no longer used. Sport hasn't been 'natural' since the first naked Olympian put on sandals. A Nautilus machine isn't natural. Should athletes train only by lifting rocks?"

Steroid use undermines the integrity of the sport. "That's the Bob Costas argument about the validity of records. There already is no validity in comparing athletes era to era. In baseball, the mound is lower, the ball livelier, the fences lower, the sizes of the fields and the rules of play are different. And what do you do about Coors Field?"

Columnist George Will wrote: "Sport—and a society that takes it seriously—would be debased if it did not strictly forbid things that blur the distinction between the triumph of character and the triumph of pharmacology."

"Did Barry Bonds undermine the integrity of baseball?" Fost asked rhetorically. "Well, the fans didn't seem to think so." And, a listener noted, the home run race between McGwire and Sosa is widely credited with bringing fans back after the strike.

"Bingo," Fost said.

Steroid users are bad role models for kids. "I'm more concerned about sexual assault, drunk driving and other things kids see some athletes doing."

Lyle Alzado

What about Lyle Alzado? "That question seems to come up every time I do an interview," Fost said. Lyle Alzado, a star defensive end in the NFL, became the poster boy for the dangers of taking steroids because of his death from brain cancer at age 42, a cancer he claimed was brought on by steroid use. So compelling was his story that, now, 16 years after his death, many websites about him conclude by saying: "Cause of death: Brain cancer brought on by excessive steroid use." "But there's not a shred of evidence to prove that connection," Fost said. "He was the poster boy for the wrong thing."

> "A little-noticed batch of new research from Sweden suggests that anyone who takes steroids, even once, may effectively be a cheater for life."

Cheaters Do Prosper

Reed Albergotti

Reed Albergotti is a reporter for the Wall Street Journal. *In the following viewpoint, he reports that a 2006 report by the Department of Integrative Medical Biology at Sweden's Umea University finds that athletes who take steroids have an unfair physical advantage over those athletes who do not take such substances—even long after an athlete quits using steroids. The study shows, Albergotti explains, that steroids change an athlete's body forever, particularly the ability to produce muscle. These lasting benefits mean that professional sports leagues should consider imposing a lifetime ban on athletes who use steroids because letting them compete is unfair and hurts the integrity of the game.*

As you read, consider the following questions:

1. According to the author, in what year did a maximum four-year ban for first-time offenders caught using performance-enhancing drugs go into effect for Olympic events?

2. According to Charles Yesalis, as cited in the viewpoint, how much of their gains from doping can athletes who continue to train retain?

3. According to George Mitchell's report on steroid use in Major League Baseball cited by Albergotti, how much improvement in production was there in players who used steroids from ages twenty-eight to thirty-four?

Scientists in Sweden make a stunning claim: The benefits of steroids may never go away—even when athletes quit taking them.

Should athletes who take steroids be banned for life?

As Major League Baseball officials discuss ways to strengthen their doping policies, there's one possibility that's not on the table—a lifetime ban for all players who are caught taking steroids. But a little-noticed batch of new research from Sweden suggests that anyone who takes steroids, even once, may effectively be a cheater for life.

In the study, which was completed in October 2006 by the Department of Integrative Medical Biology at Sweden's Umea University, researchers took muscle biopsies from 26 elite powerlifters who have competed at the sport's highest levels. Ten of the volunteers said they were not steroid users, but the other 16 had either admitted using these drugs in the past or said they were currently using them. Not only is it unusual for scientists to study elite athletes of any kind, it's almost impossible to study top athletes who are using steroids in competition.

When the researchers looked at the subjects' muscles through a microscope, they made a surprising discovery: Rather than returning to their original proportions, the muscles of the steroid users who'd stopped taking the drug looked remarkably similar to those of the subjects who were still using. They also had larger muscle fibers and more growth-inducing "myonuclei" in their muscle cells than the nonsteroid users.

A scientific consensus on this issue may be a long way off. The Swedish study was too small to be definitive, and it's difficult (for obvious reasons) to do a large follow-up study on the effects of steroids on competitive athletes. Some studies done in the past decade have shown that while the muscles of mice grow when they are given steroids, they also shrink when the drugs are taken away. Gary Wadler, a New York University physician who consults with WADA on steroid issues, says he isn't convinced that the conclusions are accurate. "The effects of steroids are time-limited," he says.

The study, which is posted on the university's website, received scant attention outside Sweden and wasn't published in a peer-reviewed journal. But researchers at Umea University presented it to Swedish doping officials and sent bound copies to both the International Olympic Committee and WADA, where it made its way into discussions of the scientific and executive committees.

At a meeting in Madrid in November, WADA's Foundation Board voted to change its code to allow for a maximum four-year ban for first-time offenders caught using performance-enhancing drugs. The new ban, which goes into effect in all sanctioned Olympic events in 2009, is a severe penalty for athletes—whose careers tend to be short. Bengt Eriksson, the vice chairman of the Swedish Sports Confederation's doping commission, who attended the Madrid conference, says he thinks the study was "one of the main reasons" WADA raised the maximum penalty. David Howman, WADA's director gen-

"Sign on baseball cage 'Do Not Feed the Ballplayers Steroids,'" cartoon by Bob Eckstein, www.CartoonStock.com. Copyright © by Bob Eckstein. Reproduction rights obtainable from www.CartoonStock.com.

eral, says the Swedish study played only a minor role in the decision. In any case, the study affirmed something a handful of scientists, athletes and strength coaches have long believed—that steroids change you forever.

The scientific understanding of steroids took a giant leap forward in 1996 when Shalender Bhasin, now chief of endocrinology, diabetes and nutrition at the Boston Medical Center, published a study in the *New England Journal of Medicine* that concluded, to the surprise of many, that steroids have a profound impact on muscle cells—even in people who take them without lifting weights. The Swedish study was inspired by a study in 1999 by Fawzi Kadi, a physiology professor at Örebro University in Switzerland, who looked at muscle biopsies from powerlifters who admitted they were taking steroids at the time of the study. (He found the muscle fibers of these subjects had ballooned well beyond normal levels.) Mr. Kadi helped guide the 2006 Swedish study, which used similar methods.

The idea that steroids may have lasting benefits comes as no surprise to Larry Maile, president of USA Powerlifting. He says former steroid-using competitors who rehabilitate themselves often become top performers. "They're still bigger and stronger than they ever would have been," he says. There is no way to prove that they're still benefiting from their years of steroid use, he adds, but the question remains, "would they really have been that good had they never used?"

Charles Yesalis, a former strength coach and professor emeritus of health policy and administration at Pennsylvania State University, says athletes who continue to train can retain as much as 85% of their gains from using drugs. This isn't based on muscle biopsies or peer-reviewed research, he says, but on 30 years of experience with athletes. He says he has talked privately with hundreds of dopers, some of them champions, and has seen the permanent benefits of performance-enhancing drugs. "These things are like rocket fuel," he says.

While many sports have had athletes test positive for steroids, baseball has become the leading case study. In December, Sen. George Mitchell released a report, prepared at baseball's request, on the prevalence of performance-enhancing drugs in the game. The report revealed the names of more than 80 players who allegedly purchased or used steroids or human growth hormone.

The report included the names of several marquee players like pitcher Roger Clemens, who denies taking the drugs. Following the report, officials from Major League Baseball and the players' union have begun intensive talks on implementing a stricter drug policy, but officials say the league isn't considering steeper punishments. Baseball's current program includes a lifetime ban only for players who test positive for steroids three times. An MLB spokesman says the league isn't aware of the research done on powerlifters and hasn't considered it during deliberations. The players' union declined to comment about the negotiations.

Because of the number of current and former players who have been implicated as steroid users or have admitted to taking the drug, baseball is the only sport where it's possible to make some rudimentary measurements of the effects of steroids on a player's performance.

When the career statistics of 52 hitters who were cited in Sen. Mitchell's report (or have been alleged to be steroid users by other sources) are measured against the average career statistics for all hitters, there are some substantial differences. For the alleged steroid users, there was a 5.4% improvement in production from ages 28 to 34 based on OPS (on-base percentage plus slugging percentage) while the average for all players between 1921–2004 who played at least 10 seasons in the majors was a 2.6% decline over that period.

It's unlikely many sports organizations will impose lifetime bans on onetime users. Travis Tygart, head of the U.S. Anti-Doping Agency, says he supports the standard two-year ban and says the new option for four years is good enough. "I could understand why athletes who are clean would want a lifetime ban," he says. "But we're comfortable with what the world has agreed to."

Nevertheless, WADA's Mr. Howman says that if science continues to confirm the findings of the Swedish study, a lifetime ban is not out of the question. "Never say never," he says. —Russell Adams contributed to this article.

> *"The importance of athletes' heads and hearts can't be underestimated—both figuratively and literally."*

Professional Sports Organizations Have a Responsibility to Safeguard the Health of Players

Jed Hughes

Jed Hughes is vice chairman of Korn/Ferry International, an executive search firm. In the following viewpoint, he maintains that sports organizations have the obligation to safeguard the health of their players, particularly when it comes to the dangers of head injuries and heart conditions. Hughes argues that with the resources that professional sports organizations have, which include excellent health care and state-of-the-art technology, a system should be implemented to monitor athletes' health and provide the best care available. Hughes concludes that regular physicals that include head and heart tests should be integral to that process.

As you read, consider the following questions:

1. What former Chicago Bears quarterback does Hughes identify as suffering from short-term memory loss?

2. What two famous American athletes may be able to pinpoint their physical declines to head injuries, according to the author?

3. According to Hughes, what was the cause of Reggie Lewis's death?

We have so many clichés in sports about head and heart. "Get your head in the game. . . . Keep your head up. . . . You gotta have heart. . . . They played with a lot of heart today. . . ." However, the importance of athletes' heads and hearts can't be underestimated—both figuratively and literally.

Head Injuries

An often overlooked aspect in sports has been the long-term impact head injuries take on an athlete's life. There is no shortage of notable athletes who were forced into early retirement due to recurrent concussions. Many of them face long-term physical difficulties and shorter life expectancies.

Head injuries are devastating. John Mackey, a top tight end for the [Baltimore] Colts and the first president of the NFL [National Football League] Players Association after the NFL-AFL [American Football League] merger, suffered from frontal temporal dementia, and spent the conclusion of his life in an assisted living facility. Former [Chicago] Bears quarterback Jim McMahon suffers from short-term memory loss and believes that his problems are related to head injuries he sustained during his career. The NFL is currently facing multimillion-dollar lawsuits filed by players who claim head trauma caused long-term damage.

Hockey players suffer more than their fair share of head trauma. Pittsburgh Penguins captain Sidney Crosby, the marquee player of the NHL [National Hockey League], has battled post-concussion syndrome for much of the past two years. After a brief return in December [2011], he sat out until March and is now playing again. There is a real possibility that his next head injury could end his career and possibly cause permanent damage. Post-concussion syndrome forced Pat LaFontaine, one of the greatest U.S.-born players, to abruptly end his Hall of Fame career. He is now an advocate for the NHL Players' Association. Eric Lindros, the #1 [NHL] pick overall in 1992, famously suffered multiple head injuries that also resulted in an early retirement.

Two of the most famous athletes in American history may be able to pinpoint their physical declines to repeated head injuries. Muhammad Ali's Parkinson's disease is very likely a result of too many blows to the head during his boxing career. A 2010 report by CNN suggested that New York Yankees legend Lou Gehrig may have fallen victim to amyotrophic lateral sclerosis (ALS) due to head injuries he incurred during a career in an era when players did not use batting helmets.

Understanding how head injuries impact athletes' long-term health is essential. Recently, [professional basketball player] Lebron James said he was "too tough to get a concussion." This kind of attitude is dangerous. We simply don't know the repercussions of head injuries sustained by adults and children who play sports. It is best to err on the side of caution when returning from concussions.

Heart Injuries

Generally, athletes are in remarkable physical shape and look and feel indestructible. Yet, there have been so many tragic examples of young athletes suffering from heart attacks and dying of heatstroke after being pushed too hard.

According to the National Center for Catastrophic Sport Injury Research at the University of North Carolina, dozens of football players have died from heatstroke since the mid-

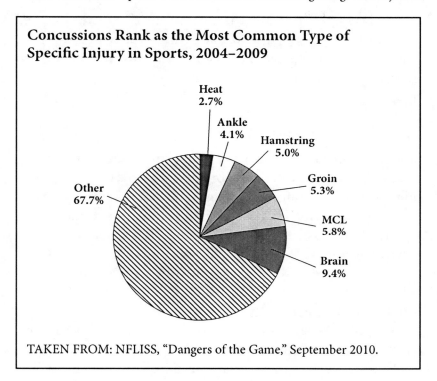

Concussions Rank as the Most Common Type of Specific Injury in Sports, 2004–2009

Heat
2.7%

Ankle
4.1%

Hamstring
5.0%

Groin
5.3%

Other
67.7%

MCL
5.8%

Brain
9.4%

TAKEN FROM: NFLISS, "Dangers of the Game," September 2010.

1990s. More than 30 of them were high school athletes. The old-school mentality of "suck it up, you are fine," can be dangerous, especially for student-athletes.

Last month [March 2012], 23-year-old Fabrice Muamba of the English Premier League's Bolton [Wanderers Football Club] went into cardiac arrest during the first half of a soccer match against Tottenham [Hotspur Football Club]. The young soccer star is lucky to have survived. Sevilla's Antonio Puerta, who died after suffering a heart attack during a Spanish League match in 2007, and Cameroon soccer star Marc-Vivien Foé, who died while playing in a match against Colombia in 2003, were not as fortunate.

In the U.S., Emily Adamczak, a high school freshman at Akron Central, died from cardiac arrest on the soccer field. Nearly five minutes had passed before she was given CPR by a bystander. Swifter response might have saved her.

Perhaps the most famous case of heart failure occurred when Reggie Lewis of the Boston Celtics dropped dead on the court during an off-season practice. He was diagnosed with hypertrophic cardiomyopathy, a fairly common heart condition.

Providing Top-Notch Care

Sports organizations have a responsibility to safeguard the health of their players. Chief among them are head and heart injuries. Unlike sprains and breaks, we cannot always see what has happened, which makes the injuries that much more dangerous. With state-of-the-art technology and superlative health services at our fingertips, isn't it time we implement a system to prevent tragedies through a process of prescreening athletes' health and assuring the best health assistance is available before taking the field?

Any athlete—amateur or professional—should have regular physicals that include head and heart tests.

Having been a coach for a long time, I've seen the effects of head injuries on players who returned to action too quickly. As a father whose son has experienced a serious concussion, I am an advocate of baseline testing followed by a procedure that determines when it is safe to return to action.

Parents must be aware of the effects of head trauma and must take advantage of the latest advances in testing for concussions. They also must heed the advice of experts before allowing their children to compete again. When it comes to brain injuries, it's always better to be safe than sorry.

> "In the macho, less-than-enlightened Republic of Sports, depression and other mental illnesses are often stigmatized as maladies for the weak."

Examining Death of Denver Broncos' Kenny McKinley

Jon Wertheim

Jon Wertheim is an author, sports journalist, and columnist for Sports Illustrated. In the following viewpoint, he finds that mental health problems are common among professional athletes, but that such ailments are stigmatized and neglected by sports organizations. Wertheim argues that as mental health becomes better understood, the culture of professional sports will change. It is inevitable, Wertheim maintains, that the stigma surrounding mental health in sports will disappear. In the meantime, he contends, professional sports organizations should take the lead, educating athletes and making mental health care available to all pro athletes.

As you read, consider the following questions:

1. According to the National Institute of Mental Health, what percentage of people who commit suicide have the risk factors for suicide?

Jon Wertheim, "Examining Death of Denver Broncos' Kenny McKinley," *Sports Illustrated*, September 21, 2010. Copyright © 2010 by Time Inc. A Time Warner Company. All rights reserved. Reproduced by permission.

2. According to studies, how likely is it for someone who has had multiple concussions to suffer from depression?

3. According to the National Institute of Mental Health, what percentage of American adults suffer from a diagnosable mental disorder every year?

McKinley's apparent suicide casts light on athletes' risk of depression.

Story Highlights

- Broncos' Kenny McKinley found dead on Monday of a self-inflicted gunshot wound.

- Athletes are supposed to be macho, so mental illness is often looked down upon.

- In a high-stress environment, pressure can get to even the strongest individuals.

It was before the famous tent stint in Australia, the various drug suspensions, the holistic medicine, the Toronto Argonauts and the Redemption. In the summer of 2003, Ricky Williams was passing through New York on a media tour and we ended up talking. Williams said a few words about his football career, but then, candid as ever, he took the conversation on a hairpin turn and began to talk about his battles with mental illness.

You may recall that during his fairly disastrous tenure with the New Orleans Saints, Williams had a habit of answering questions without removing his football helmet. But that wasn't all. After practice, he would leave the locker room and head to the Burger King drive-thru, only to realize that he would have to interact with someone to place an order. So he would head home to spend the rest of the day in seclusion. The phone would ring and he wouldn't pick up. "At practice [the next day] my teammates would be like, 'Hey, what did you do last night?'" Williams recalled. "I'm thinking, I went from the living room to the office to the bedroom."

The team did little to help. Only after tooling around the Internet did Williams self-diagnose himself with social anxiety disorder. He finally amassed the courage to confront the Saints' hidebound coach, Jim Haslett. He explained that he was seeking treatment for a psychological issue. According to Williams, Haslett used profanity to tell him, in so many words, "to stop being a baby and just play football." (Haslett did not respond to *SI*'s questions about the incident.)

Around the same time, Williams broke his ankle. The team treated his recovery as a matter of vital importance. Trainers and rehab specialists oversaw his every move and asked for near-daily updates on his condition. Teammates texted him daily. Williams was struck by the contrast. "There's a physical prejudice in sports," he says. "When it's a broken bone, the teams will do everything in their power to make sure it's OK. When it's a broken soul, it's like a weakness."

I recalled this when the news broke that Denver Broncos wide receiver Kenny McKinley was found dead on Monday afternoon in Arapahoe County of an apparent self-inflicted gunshot wound. While the investigation is ongoing and McKinley hasn't been officially linked to depression, one has to wonder if he was depressed, especially after he was placed on injured reserve with a knee injury. (According to the National Institute of Mental Health, the risk factors for suicide include depression and other mental disorders or a substance abuse disorder. More than 90 percent of people who commit suicide have these risk factors.)

To the uninitiated, it makes no sense. Aren't these young, sculpted, famous, rich gladiators antithetical to the whole concept of depression? Aren't pro athletes supposed to be impervious to all manner of pain? Don't they collide violently against each other, and need to be talked out of playing with the kinds of injuries that would incapacitate most of us for weeks?

Recognizing the Problem

In the late 1980s a researcher at the University of Southern Maine named Loren Coleman studied the suicide patterns of MLB [Major League Baseball] players—77 current or former big leaguers had taken their own lives, more than half of them between their late 20s and late 40s—and called for an improved counseling program for retirees. The recommendation resonated loudly on July 18, 1989, when [California] Angels reliever Donnie Moore, 35, shot his wife (who survived) and killed himself at their home. Moore, a former all-star who had been released from Triple A the previous month, had given up a series-turning homer to the Red Sox's Dave Henderson in the top of the ninth inning in Game 5 of the 1986 ALCS [American League Championship Series]. Friends say that Moore was forever haunted by that one pitch.

Pablo S. Torre, "A Light in the Darkness,"
Sports Illustrated, June 21, 2010.

In the macho, less-than-enlightened Republic of Sports, depression and other mental illnesses are often stigmatized as maladies for the weak. "Gutless" was the term Bobby Valentine, then the Mets manager, allegedly used to describe Pete Harnisch after the pitcher suffered a depressive episode. "Run it off," an NBA coach once told Vin Baker when the player tried to explain his depression. "Don't let the blues get you down!"

"Head case" remains one of the most damning labels in the front office. Sports psychologists know that if they want acceptance among athletes, they're better off re-branding themselves as the less menacing "performance coaches."

The abiding irony: It's entirely possible that athletes in pro sports—the ultimate kennel of alpha dogs—might be MORE prone to mental illness than members of society at large. After hereditary influences, the biggest risk factor for depression is stress. Performing in front of thousands of fans, having your work scrutinized and judged regularly, and laboring in a field where success and failure are so clear-cut can exact a huge psychic toll. There's also the stress of knowing that your career, and thus the window of opportunity to make millions, is narrow. As McKinley's agent, Andrew Bondarowicz, told the *Denver Post*: "These guys, they're made of steel on the outside. But for a lot of them, the challenge of being at your best and living up to all the expectations is a difficult situation. Some people are better equipped and have the support system."

Other factors include:

• Head injuries. Studies show that someone who has endured multiple concussions is up to four times more likely to suffer depression. Athletes, of course, are at a far greater risk than the general population to suffer cranial injuries, which can alter brain chemistry. Andre Waters, the Eagles' fearsome defensive back, committed suicide in 2006 at age 43; an autopsy revealed that his brain tissue had degenerated to that befitting a man in his 80s.

Another Philadelphia football player, Owen Thomas, a reserve for Penn, committed suicide in April and was honored posthumously just last weekend. According to researchers, he, too, showed early signs of chronic traumatic encephalopathy.

• Childhood trauma. Researchers know that exposure to trauma at a young age can lead to an increased likelihood of depression and mental illness later in life. (Studies have also shown that growing up in a single-parent household can increase the risk.) Think about how many "athlete narratives" contain almost unimaginably bleak childhood episodes.

Apart from medication and therapy, mental health can be improved by social stability and a solid home life. For all the perks of playing sports for a living, social stability does not rank high on the list. From the road games to the constant possibility of a trade to an all-consuming regular season to the dissonance that accompanies coming into vast sums of wealth overnight, sports are hardly conducive to social stability.

The wheels of progress tend to turn slowly in sports. But they do rotate. As mental health has become better understood and accepted in the mainstream—where the National Institute of Mental Health suggests that a quarter of American adults suffer from a diagnosable mental disorder in a given year—so too are psychological issues beginning to lose some of their stigma in sports. In recent years a welter of athletes in a variety of sports (Jennifer Capriati, Joey Votto, Stephane Richer) have unashamedly admitted to battling mental illness. It was the inimitable Ron Artest who, during his memorable monologue after the NBA Finals, expressed profuse thanks to his psychiatrist.

In this excellent recent article, my colleague Pablo Torre notes that Royals pitcher Zack Greinke is even hailed as the "Jackie Robinson" of mental illness. Greinke missed most of an entire season to address and treat social anxiety disorder and clinical depression. Crediting therapy and antidepressants, he returned to win the Cy Young Award. "Whether he likes it or not, [Greinke] is the guy who really paved the way for the modern player to come out about these issues," Mike Sweeney, a former teammate, told *SI*.

Scan the injured reserve or disabled list and, likely for the first time, explanations of "social anxiety" and "stress related" are among the listed causes. To Ricky Williams's point, athletes now can have a credible reason for missing games even if the malady doesn't appear on an X-ray or MRI.

In some cases, teams and leagues and even college programs have gone proactive, educating athletes and making psychiatrists, psychologists and mental health experts readily available. In Torre's story, source after source suggested that the culture in sports is, finally, shifting. As it should be. Athletes like Kenny McKinley might appear to be made of steel on the outside. Inside? They're simply as prone to mental illness as the rest of us—likely more so.

"The recent emphasis on concussions has been a major impetus in the altering of rules regarding questionable hits."

Is Pro Football Too Dangerous?

Stu Durando

Stu Durando is a sportswriter for the St. Louis Post-Dispatch. *In the following viewpoint, he reports that despite attempts to clearly outline the rules for safe play in the National Football League (NFL), confusion still abounds over what is a dangerous hit on a player and what is an acceptable one. Durando finds that many officials are hopeful that the league's stricter approach to head and neck injuries will result in fewer career-ending injuries and will protect players from dangerous concussions. The NFL must go further and clarify the rules even more, Durando contends, especially when it comes to hits on defenseless players, and they should continue to focus on decreasing the number of concussions to players in order to protect a player's long-term health.*

As you read, consider the following questions:

1. According to an NFL study, how many retired players reported that they suffered from dementia, Alzheimer's disease, and other memory-related issues?

2. How much does the author say that Dunta Robinson was fined for a vicious hit on DeSean Jackson?

3. According to a 2010 Harris public opinion poll, what percentage of Americans believe that players who cause head injuries should face penalties such as suspension?

Fines levied against NFL players were rampant before mid-season, with five-figure penalties becoming common occurrences. Suspensions were threatened. And the debate over safety measures had become heated.

So last month, the NFL released 11 pages of previously private information. Taken from the league's policy manual distributed to players, the guidelines were unveiled to shed light on rules that are behind a story that has dominated the 2010 season.

With the emphasis on safety at an all-time high, the document revealed what players are supposed to know when it comes to hits that are acceptable and those that cross the ever-thinning line between good and evil.

The rules are spelled out in detail with the help of occasional boldfaced text and five illustrations, which depict unacceptable contact and emphasize the point of contact with cartoon-like symbols.

Yet, confusion continues to rage even as the NFL reviews every play from every game in a full-throttle attempt to eliminate neck and head contact on "defenseless players."

Fines for such hits have poured out of the NFL office in recent months, including four totaling $125,000 addressed to Pittsburgh's James Harrison. The NFL responded to a batch of incidents one week by issuing an edict that penalties would become more severe if "devastating hits and head shots" didn't stop.

"Everyone wants to be safe and no one wants to hurt each other, but then again, this is a violent game," Rams player representative Adam Goldberg said. "If we were playing two-hand touch, no one would watch. It's a fine line, and I think the league is trying to move that line this year."

The increased emphasis on player protection came after the institution of new guidelines on concussions and an NFL study that revealed an array of medical problems suffered by former players.

The discussion has generated a trickle-down effect, not only to college and high school football but to youth organizations that are addressing how they handle the game's inherent violence and head injuries.

The NFL has made its loudest statement yet this season. Some offenses fall into the clear-cut category of helmet-to-helmet contact. Others are more subjective and involve hits on "defenseless" players, a term that is defined in the player manual and has been expanded on the college level.

Conflicting Perspectives

Some players have been critical of the NFL's tough stand, but retired cornerback Aeneas Williams suggested they ultimately will adjust and reap the benefits not afforded to those who have left the game.

"The current guys don't understand the enormous risk that's involved because they haven't retired," he said. "There's a generation that's retired and starting to see the ramifications of hits that once were considered glorious and, quite frankly, were part of the promotion of the game.

"Guys who are recently retired are less likely to admit things they're going through. But you may be in your mid-30s and all of a sudden you're dealing with things you can't remember."

NFL commissioner Roger Goodell testified before the House Judiciary Committee in October 2009 and provided information on the league's survey of retired players. He said of 1,070 who were contacted, 56 reported that they suffered from dementia, Alzheimer's disease and other memory-related issues.

The league has a medical plan that provides coverage for former players diagnosed with dementia and has expanded it to include benefits for those with ALS, also known as Lou Gehrig's Disease.

Concussions at the Forefront

The recent emphasis on concussions has been a major impetus in the altering of rules regarding questionable hits. As research produced a greater understanding of the long-term impact, officials at all levels took action.

The NFL does not allow players who suffer concussions to return to practice or a game on the same day. They must be symptom-free and pass numerous tests before being cleared to play.

The National Federation of State High School Associations passed a similar rule this year. Washington became the first state to pass a law regarding concussions after a 13-year-old suffered a serious head injury while playing football. And Pop Warner youth football announced that it will require medical clearance before a player can return from a head injury.

Dr. Mark Halstead, director of the sports concussion program with Washington University and a Rams team doctor, released a report on concussions in children this year. He said as recently as 10 years ago, high school players with concussion symptoms would be allowed to return to action as soon as they felt better.

But there is evidence that even youth athletes might suffer long-term effects from head injuries. Halstead noted in his report that an autopsy on the brain of an 18-year-old athlete with a history of concussions showed signs of chronic traumatic encephalopathy, which had previously been detected only in pro football players and boxers.

"We don't know what the findings on the brain mean in terms of symptoms," he said. "But a lot of former NFL athletes have been suffering from depression, significant emotional problems and additional issues. We don't know how much can be attributed to the findings in the brain."

Time to Take Action

The NFL isn't waiting to find out. Fines have been common this season, but the sense of urgency escalated after a series of well-publicized hits on Oct. 17.

Harrison was fined $75,000 for a hit on Cleveland's Mohamed Massaquoi. A head-to-head hit cost New England's Brandon Meriweather $50,000. Atlanta's Dunta Robinson also received a bill for $50,000 after a vicious hit on Philadelphia's DeSean Jackson.

Days later, NFL vice president of football operations Ray Anderson issued a stern statement.

"We can't and won't tolerate what we saw Sunday," he wrote. "We've got to get the message to players that these devastating hits and head shots will be met with a very necessary higher standard of accountability. . . . We're talking about avoiding life-altering impacts."

Many players have voiced confusion about what is acceptable and what isn't. Part of the problem is that referees must translate the meaning of "defenseless."

In its definition of "defenseless positions" the NFL cites quarterbacks in the act of passing, receivers in the process of making a catch, a runner whose forward progress is stopped and in the grasp of a tackler, a return man fielding a kick and a player on the ground at the end of a play.

"Some of the hits may seem more vicious, more malicious," Rams cornerback Ron Bartell said, "but it's always been the case. They should have concerns. Head injuries are a big deal. But you have to be realistic. You can't ask guys to make a decision on how they tackle in a split second."

Some fines have come for plays that weren't penalized during the game. But the glaring infraction of leading with the head and initiating helmet-to-helmet contact has become a major focus.

Improving Safety

The NFL has long had a head, neck and spine committee. This week the group held meetings in New York, where it met with officials from NASCAR and the military, among other groups, to discuss ways to improve head safety.

"There's no question that what has evolved is the notion that a helmet can be an offensive weapon," said Dr. Robert Cantu, professor of neurosurgery at Boston University and the senior adviser for the committee. "That's what the commissioner is trying to change. It won't happen in one year, but when people get suspended for helmet-to-helmet hits, you might see a change in attitude."

The recent paralysis suffered by Rutgers player Eric LeGrand was a jarring reminder of the danger of the sport.

Spectacular hits by defensive players on ball carriers were once celebrated in the NFL much like the dunk in the NBA. ESPN aired a segment called "Jacked Up" for several years, ending in 2006, reviewing the week's hardest hits.

When the Harris Poll conducted a survey on football this year, 58 percent of respondents said players who cause head injuries should face penalties such as suspension.

Over time, the NFL has adopted many rule changes designed to reduce the danger. In 1979, players on the receiving team were prohibited from blocking below the waist on kickoff and punt returns. A personal foul was instituted in 1996 for hits with the helmet or to the head. And in 2005, the "horse collar" tackle was banned.

Colleges Take Notice

The college game has kept pace and this year placed a greater emphasis on penalizing hits on defenseless players. Bill Carollo, coordinator of officials for the Big Ten, Mid-American and Missouri Valley conferences, sends a training video to his referees each week, and roughly one-third of the plays are related to player safety.

"In deciding when a player is defenseless, we've told the officials, coaches and the athletic directors we're going to err on the side of safety," Carollo said. "I want our accuracy to be 96 percent or higher when we throw a flag. For unnecessary roughness—I don't like it—but I will accept 90 percent."

Although there were no college rule changes this season regarding safety, the emphasis was changed to include contact to the head with a forearm, elbow or shoulder. Carollo said the number of helmet-to-helmet hits was reduced significantly this season.

Meanwhile, the NFL is looking for a similar result, but the fines continue to pile up. In recent weeks, Baltimore's Jameel McClain was fined $40,000 for a helmet hit, Detroit's Ndamukong Suh was fined $15,000 for pushing a quarterback and Philadelphia's Trent Cole was fined $20,000 for a knee hit.

"Everyone has a job to do," Goldberg said. "Everyone is trying to do what they can in their power to make the game safer. Whether it's right or wrong is not really my place to say. Safety is a priority for all sides."

> *"The [National Football League] likes to say that views about concussions have shifted from simply accepting they're part of the sport to doing what's possible to lessen impacts."*

Some NFL Players Still Willing to Hide Concussions

Howard Fendrich

Howard Fendrich is a reporter for the Associated Press. In the following viewpoint, he finds that a majority of players in the National Football League (NFL) would hide a concussion from coaches and trainers rather than report it. Fendrich reports that although these players are largely aware of the possible long-term effects of concussions and the risk of playing with one, they accept that it is part of the game and would rather be out on the field than sitting on the bench. Furthermore, Fendrich explains, these players argue that their competitive instinct and insecurity over their place on the team cause them to hide injuries or downplay them to get back on the field. To change this culture, he concludes, the NFL needs to continue its efforts to educate players on the risks and effects of concussions and have physicians who are not affiliated with the team evaluate head injuries.

As you read, consider the following questions:

1. According to a series of interviews by the Associated Press cited in the viewpoint, how many NFL players said they would try to conceal a possible concussion?

2. According to interviews cited by Fendrich, how many players out of forty-four said that the NFL should have independent neurologists at games to evaluate head injuries?

3. According to data from STATS LLC cited in the viewpoint, how many NFL players went on injured reserve because of a concussion or head injury in the 2010–2011 season?

A sk Jacksonville Jaguars running back Maurice Jones-Drew whether he would try to play through a concussion or yank himself from a game, and he'll provide a straightforward answer.

"Hide it," the NFL's leading rusher said.

"The bottom line is: You have to be able to put food on the table. No one's going to sign or want a guy who can't stay healthy. I know there will be a day when I'm going to have trouble walking. I realize that," Jones-Drew said. "But this is what I signed up for. Injuries are part of the game. If you don't want to get hit, then you shouldn't be playing."

Other players say they would do the same: Hide it.

In a series of interviews about head injuries with the Associated Press over the last two weeks, 23 of 44 NFL players—slightly more than half—said they would try to conceal a possible concussion rather than pull themselves out of a game. Some acknowledged they already have. Players also said they should be better protected from their own instincts: More than two-thirds of the group the AP talked to wants independent neurologists on sidelines during games.

The AP spoke to a cross-section of players—at least one from each of the 32 NFL teams—to gauge whether concussion safety and attitudes about head injuries have changed in the past two years of close attention devoted to the issue. The group included 33 starters and 11 reserves; 25 players on offense and 19 on defense; all have played at least three seasons in the NFL.

The players tended to indicate they are more aware of the possible long-term effects of jarring hits to their heads than they once were. In a sign of the sort of progress the league wants, five players said that while they would have tried to conceal a concussion during a game in 2009, now they would seek help.

"You look at some of the cases where you see some of the retired players and the issues that they're having now, even with some of the guys who've passed and had their brains examined—you see what their brains look like now," said Washington Redskins linebacker London Fletcher, the NFL's leading tackler. "That does play a part in how I think now about it."

But his teammate, backup fullback Mike Sellers, said he's hidden concussions in the past and would "highly doubt" that any player would willingly take himself out of a game.

"You want to continue to play. You're a competitor. You're not going to tell on yourself. There have been times I've been dinged, and they've taken my helmet from me, and . . . I'd snatch my helmet back and get back on the field," Sellers said. "A lot of guys wouldn't say anything because a lot of guys wouldn't think anything during the game, until afterward, when they have a headache or they can't remember certain things."

San Francisco 49ers defensive lineman Justin Smith captured a popular sentiment: Players know of the potential problems, yet would risk further damage.

"It doesn't take a rocket scientist to figure out if (you have) a concussion, you're probably damaging your brain a little bit. Just like if you sprain your wrist a bunch, you're going to have some wrist problems down the road. Yeah, I'd still play through it. It's part of it. It's part of the game," Smith said. "I think if you're noticeably messed up, yeah, they'll take you out. But if you've just got some blurry vision, I'd say that's the player's call. And most guys—99 percent of guys in the NFL—are going to play through it."

Smith said he sustained one concussion in high school ("You don't know who you are," is how he described it) and another in college ("Walking around the whole time, but I don't remember anything until six hours later").

The NFL likes to say that views about concussions have shifted from simply accepting they're part of the sport to doing what's possible to lessen impacts. Commissioner Roger Goodell talks about "changing the culture," so players don't try to "walk it off" after taking hits to the head.

Yet the AP's conversations with players showed there is room for more adjustments, which did not surprise Dr. Richard Ellenbogen, co-chairman of the NFL's head, neck and spine committee.

"The culture change takes a while," Ellenbogen said in a telephone interview. "Why would these guys want to go out? They love playing the game. They don't want to leave their team. They want to win. I understand all that. And that's why we have to be on our toes with coming up with exams that are hard to beat, so to speak."

New Orleans Saints offensive lineman Zach Strief put it this way: "We all grew up with, 'Hey, get back in there. You (only) got your bell rung.' And while it's changing now, I think it's going to take time for the mind-set to change."

A few players said they'd be particularly inclined to hide a concussion if it happened in a play-off game or the Super Bowl. Some said their decision would depend on the severity of a head injury—but they'd hide it if they could.

Clearly, there is a stigma associated with leaving the field, no matter the reason. Indeed, one player who said he'd exit a game if he thought he might have a concussion didn't want to be quoted on the subject.

Other findings from the interviews:

—Asked whether the NFL should have independent neurologists at games to examine players and determine if they should be held out because of concussions, 31 players said "yes," and 10 said "no." Three didn't answer.

"They've got guys looking at your uniform to make sure you're wearing the right kind of socks," St. Louis Rams safety Quintin Mikell said. "Why not have somebody there to protect your head? I think we definitely should have that."

He said he's tried to clear his head and stay on the field "many times."

"I'll probably pay for it later in my life," Mikell said, "but at the same time, I'll probably pay for the alcohol that I drank or driving fast cars. It's one of those things that it just comes with the territory."

—Specifically regarding concussions, 28 of the 44 players think playing in the NFL is safer now than in 2009, while 13 think it's the same, and two think it's more dangerous. One wasn't sure. Those who think safety has improved gave credit to the rise in awareness; more fines for illegal hits; this season's changes to kickoff rules that have cut down on the number of returns; and the new labor contract's reduction in the amount of contact allowed in practice.

"When I first came into the league, it was like, 'Whatever goes.' It was more of that old-school, just 'beat-him-up' football. Not wanting to hurt anybody, but show how tough you were. Back in the day, it was like if you come out (of a game) with (a) slight concussion, then you weren't giving it all for your team," Buffalo Bills linebacker Andra Davis said. "But now, they're taking that option away from you."

Davis, a 10th-year veteran who turned 33 on Friday and said he's had a couple of concussions, is one of those whose view on seeking help for such injuries has changed.

"The younger me would definitely hide it," Davis said. "But the older me now—with a wife and kids and looking more at life after football—I would say something about it."

—Asked whether more can be done to protect players from head injuries, 18 players said "yes," and 24 said "no." Two did not respond.

Not surprisingly, there were divisions according to position, and players on opposite sides of the ball generally drifted toward opposing views: Those on offense seemed more likely than those on defense to say more can—and should—be done to improve safety. Linemen, meanwhile, often complained that there is no way to improve their plight, with the helmet-to-helmet banging that takes place at the snap on play after play. One player described those collisions as "micro-episodes that build up over time."

Nearly three-quarters of the players who told the AP they think safety can improve—13 of 18—suggested equipment can be improved, too. Helmet technology, mouth guards and chin straps all were mentioned.

Two players suggested more education about concussions is needed.

Dr. Robert Cantu, a senior adviser to Ellenbogen's NFL committee who said he is consulted regularly by the league, insisted that while there has been progress, there is still work to be done.

"Has there been a culture change overall? I think the answer is, unquestionably, 'yes.' Could there be more done? Yes. Do all the players get it? No. Do they want to get it? No," said Cantu, a clinical professor of neurosurgery and codirector of the Center for the Study of Traumatic Encephalopathy at Boston University School of Medicine.

CTE is a degenerative disease increasingly found in football players and other athletes who have absorbed repeated blows to the head. It has been linked to memory loss, disorientation, poor decision making, and depression that can lead to drug use and, as in the case of former Chicago Bears defensive back Dave Duerson, even suicide.

The league distributed informational posters in 2010 to warn about the dangers of head injuries, but Cantu said: "Just because the posters are in every locker room, it's not mandatory reading. Or people can say they read it but not really have read it."

"More stress needs to be placed—and I believe this is the players' association's responsibility as much as it is the NFL's—on the dangers of playing symptomatic with a concussion and more knowledge needs to be imparted on chronic traumatic encephalopathy, which obviously does exist in the NFL. . . . All of those sub-concussive blows count, and you need to minimize the amount of brain trauma that you take," Cantu said.

Union spokesman George Atallah declined a request for comment about concussions.

Little-discussed until reporting by the *New York Times* led to an October 2009 congressional hearing on concussions in the NFL, head injuries are now part of the daily conversation about professional football. On Saturday alone, two starting quarterbacks, Cleveland's Colt McCoy and Arizona's Kevin Kolb, sat out because of head injuries, while a third, Minnesota's Christian Ponder, left his team's game with what his coach called "concussion-like symptoms."

According to data from STATS LLC, from 2000–09, an average of 3.1 NFL players—and never more than nine in an entire season—went on injured reserve because of a concussion or head injury. That number rose to 18 last season and stood at 17 through Week 15 this season.

What Is a Concussion?

A concussion is a type of traumatic brain injury, or TBI, caused by a bump, blow, or jolt to the head that can change the way your brain normally works. Concussions can also occur from a blow to the body that causes the head to move rapidly back and forth. Even a "ding," "getting your bell rung," or what seems to be mild bump or blow to the head can be serious.

Concussions can occur in *any* sport or recreation activity. So, all coaches, parents, and athletes need to learn concussion signs and symptoms and what to do if a concussion occurs.

"Concussion in Sports,"
Centers for Disease Control and Prevention, July 23, 2012.

Similarly, STATS LLC said, over that same 10-year span at the start of the century, an average of 26 NFL players each season were listed on the weekly injury report and missed games because of a concussion or head injury. That number rose to 89 in 2010 and stood at 75 this season through Saturday's games.

At least eight lawsuits have been filed against the NFL in recent months—including three within the last week—by dozens of former players who say they have medical problems related to brain injuries from their time in professional football. The NFL's stance, in part, is that players knew there were risks of injury, and there was no misconduct or liability on the league's part.

"It's a physical sport. Guys are going to get hit in the head. When we're young, when we start playing this sport, we know what we're getting into," Philadelphia Eagles tight end Brent

Celek said. "It's not like, 'Oh, I'm going to play this because my head's going to be fine when I'm done playing.' It's a risk you take playing this game, but I think the league is doing everything in their power to make it as safe as possible."

The NFL certainly has found itself adjusting on the fly.

One example: After San Diego Chargers offensive lineman Kris Dielman got a concussion but stayed in the lineup in October, then had a seizure on a team flight, the NFL said it would give game officials "concussion awareness training" so they could keep an eye out for players.

A few players interviewed by the AP mentioned the recent case of Cleveland's McCoy, who has missed two consecutive games after a shot to the helmet from Pittsburgh Steelers linebacker James Harrison. McCoy was not checked for a concussion during the game against Pittsburgh and went back in; Harrison was suspended for a game; starting with this week's games, the league put certified athletic trainers in booths above the field to watch for injuries. The trainers aren't there to diagnose or prescribe treatment, the NFL said, but are supposed to call down to team medical staffs to alert them there could be a problem.

Some think the league could go further.

"I don't think it's sufficient. I think it's a great first step," BU's Cantu said, mentioning a study that showed concussions were noticed more in junior hockey when there was an observer at the rink.

While Cantu, like players interviewed by the AP, is in favor of having independent neurosurgeons at games rather than only team-employed doctors—something raised as a possibility in 2009 but never done—NFL committee co-chairman Ellenbogen said the more pressing issue was "the ability to see all the players on the field."

"Team doctors are pretty concerned about concussions, and I don't think they're people that are going to be bought and sold. . . . If the real problem is the doctors are being influenced by the coaches, then we've got to fix that," said Ellenbo-gen, chairman of the department of neurological surgery at the University of Washington School of Medicine. "If the (players' union) says, 'We want independent neurologists,' we'll discuss that. . . . To be honest with you, we ain't done. When our committee meets with the team physicians after the Super Bowl, everything's on the table. You think this is the last ren-dition of what we do? Heck, no. We're not done."

As it is, while the players the AP spoke to tend to feel bet-ter about the way concussions are handled now than in 2009, they won't deny that dangers lurk.

"You're never going to be totally safe from concussions in this game," Oakland Raiders cornerback Stanford Routt said. "This is the only place where you can actually legally assault people."

Periodical and Internet Sources Bibliography

The following articles have been selected to supplement the diverse views presented in this chapter.

Jon Baskin	"Steroids, Baseball, America," *The Point*, no. 4, Spring 2011.
Kevin Baxter	"Player Whose Career Was Ended Takes on Concussions in Soccer," *Los Angeles Times*, March 3, 2012.
Ken Belson	"For N.F.L., Concussion Suits May Be Test for Sport Itself," *New York Times*, December 29, 2011.
Laura Fitzpatrick	"Steroids," *Time*, January 13, 2010.
Norman Fost	"Handling Pro Athletes Who Use Steroids," *Washington Examiner*, October 18, 2009.
Dan Levy	"Have Professional Sports Always Been This Dangerous?," *Bleacher Report*, April 24, 2012.
Edwin Moses	"Why Baseball Is in Denial," *Newsweek*, February 20, 2009.
Anthony Papa	"Is Roger Clemens a Victim of the Drug War?," *Washington Post*, August 26, 2010.
Casey Schwartz	"Junior Seau Suicide Shows How Little We Know About Head Trauma," *The Daily Beast*, May 6, 2012.
John Stossel	"Steroids Hysteria," Townhall.com, May 6, 2009.
Paul Whitefield	"Violence, Not Replacement Refs, Will Kill the NFL," *Los Angeles Times*, September 25, 2012.
Stephen Whyno	"Concussions a Growing Problem in Hockey," *Washington Times*, February 7, 2012.

CHAPTER 3

Should Limitations Be Placed on Athletes' Free Expression?

Chapter Preface

In 2010 Tim Tebow was poised to take professional football by storm. Already renowned for his stellar college football career, Tebow was about to enter the 2010 National Football League (NFL) draft that spring. In college, he had excelled as the quarterback for the University of Florida Gators, winning two national championships and the 2007 Heisman Trophy. Some pundits argued he was one of the best college football players ever. Despite the praise for his college athletic career, many prognosticators were divided on his prospects in the pros. His supporters opined that Tebow's style of play and talent had the potential to revolutionize the game.

Off the field, Tebow ignited a raging controversy over his very public expressions of religious devotion. A staunch Christian, Tebow was very vocal about his faith and the role it played in his football career and everyday life. In January 2010, Tebow and his family decided to star in a pro-life commercial sponsored by Focus on the Family—a socially conservative Christian organization—that would air during Super Bowl XLIV and be seen by millions of people. In the ad, Tebow's mother, Pam, tells the story of her difficult pregnancy with Tim. As a Christian missionary in the Philippines, Pam had contracted dysentery and was advised to abort her fetus for health reasons. She ignored doctors' advice and gave birth to a healthy boy, Tim, on August 14, 1987.

Women's groups called for CBS, the television network broadcasting the Super Bowl, to turn down the ad. CBS refused, and the controversial commercial aired on February 7, 2010, during the Super Bowl.

Tebow was well aware that the ad would be controversial. "I know some people won't agree with it," he said in a press conference on January 24, 2010, in Mobile, Alabama, as quoted by Brinda Adhikari for *ABC World News with Diane Sawyer*.

"But I think they can at least respect that I stand up for what I believe. I've always been very convicted of [his views on abortion] because that's the reason I'm here, because my mom was a very courageous woman."

Tebow's religious expression during games also generated attention from fans and media. In 2011 fans began to post pictures on Facebook mimicking Tebow's habit of kneeling in prayer with his head resting on his fist. The pose became known as "Tebowing," and young people all over the country began to have pictures taken of themselves doing variations of Tebowing all over the world. It quickly became a popular Internet meme, and the term Tebowing entered common vernacular.

On the field, opponents began to mock Tebow with the pose. During a game in October 2011, a Detroit Lions player, Stephen Tulloch, Tebowed after tackling him for a loss. Later that same game, another Lions player, Tony Scheffler, also mocked Tebow with the pose after a scoring play.

Critics jumped on the Detroit players, accusing them of mocking Tebow's Christian religion—not the player himself. Others claimed that Tebow's very public expression of religion that took place in front of millions of people every week invited scrutiny and made him fair game for ridicule.

The issue of public religious expression in professional sports is explored in the following chapter, which focuses on the limitations on the free expression of athletes. Other viewpoints in the chapter examine the right to voice controversial opinions and the role of social media.

"The idea that one has the right to have one's own views about certain matters and to voice those views without fear of retribution is just that—an idea."

Professional Athletes and Managers Have the Right to Voice Controversial Opinions

Nsenga K. Burton

Nsenga K. Burton is a filmmaker, journalist, and editor of the Root. In the following viewpoint, she examines the controversy surrounding baseball manager Ozzie Guillén's suspension for making positive remarks about the Cuban dictator Fidel Castro during an interview. Burton argues that if freedom of speech is truly free, then Guillén has the right to have unpopular views about Castro without being suspended for expressing those views. Guillén's punishment, she contends, shows that the concept of free speech does not apply to everyone equally, and that most people cannot practice free speech without facing some sort of retribution or suppression.

As you read, consider the following questions:

1. According to Burton, what two writers did the *National Review* fire for making racially inflammatory remarks in 2012?

2. For how many games does the author say Bud Selig suspended Ozzie Guillén?

3. What percentage of players in Major League Baseball are Latino, according to the author?

My mother often says, "Free speech isn't always free." One doesn't have to look very far for real-world examples of people being made to pay for uttering, tweeting or writing words that don't sit well with various communities.

The *National Review* fired two writers within a week for making racially inflammatory comments. The conservative publication dropped John Derbyshire and Robert Weissberg— the former for a blog post demonizing blacks, and Weissberg for an incendiary talk espousing the virtues of white nationalism. Derbyshire and Weissberg aren't the only recent casualties of "free speech."

Journalist Roland Martin was suspended by CNN in February [2012] for tweets sent during the Super Bowl that GLAAD [Gay & Lesbian Alliance Against Defamation] said were homophobic. Martin denied the charge and said the tweets were misinterpreted, but he was suspended nonetheless. Scores of advertisers dumped Rush Limbaugh's radio show over his derogatory comments about Georgetown University law student Sandra Fluke. Limbaugh apologized for his sexist comments after the media firestorm. I could go on, but you get the gist.

Ozzie Guillén

Perhaps the most interesting example of the real cost of free speech is Miami Marlins manager Ozzie Guillén's most recent controversy over positive, admiring comments he made about Fidel Castro on *Time* magazine's website last week [in April 2012]. Guillén, who was suspended for five games by Commissioner of Baseball Bud Selig, apologized profusely in Spanish and English, saying that he was thinking in Spanish but used the wrong English to communicate his feelings about Castro.

Many in the Cuban community are calling for Guillén to be fired or for his resignation, while others believe that he has a right to his opinion, even if it does not sit well with Selig, Major League Baseball [MLB] or the Cuban community.

I find it preposterous that Selig—who sat with Castro during a Baltimore Orioles exhibition game against Cuba in 1999 and who refused to move the 2011 MLB All-Star Game from Phoenix, despite the controversial anti-immigrant SB [Senate Bill] 1070 law targeting Latinos in Arizona—has the nerve to feign outrage over Guillén's comments.

According to ESPN, in a statement about the suspension, Selig said, "Guillén's remarks, which were offensive to an important part of the Miami community and others throughout the world, have no place in our game." He also said that baseball as an institution has "important social responsibilities" and he expects those representing the game to show respect and sensitivity to its many cultures.

Funny, when asked about SB 1070, he said that political issues did not belong in baseball. So which is it?

A Double Standard

In addition to Selig being a complete hypocrite, Guillén's treatment speaks to the fact that there is a double standard when it comes to who really has the right to speak freely. Who is Selig to point out Guillén's responsibility to the Cuban community when he himself abdicated his responsibility to the Latino community when it suited him?

Fidel Castro and the United States

On Jan. 1, 1959, [Fidel] Castro and his July 26th movement assumed power [in Cuba], proclaimed a provisional government, and began public trials and executions of "criminals" of the [Fulgencio] Batista regime. On February 15 Castro replaced José Miró Cardona as prime minister and appointed his own brother commander of the armed forces. A powerful speaker and a charismatic leader, Castro began exerting an almost mystical hold over the Cuban masses. . . .

By the end of 1959 a radicalization of the revolution had begun to take place. Purges or defections of military leaders became common, and their replacement by more radical and oftentimes Communist militants was the norm. Newspapers critical of these new leaders were quickly silenced.

This internal trend toward a Communist agenda was reflected in foreign policy too. Castro accused the United States of harboring aggressive designs against the revolution. In February 1960 a Cuban-Soviet trade agreement was signed, and soon after Cuba established diplomatic relations with the Soviet Union and most Communist countries. Several months later, when the three largest American oil refineries in Cuba refused to refine Soviet petroleum, Castro confiscated them. The United States retaliated by cutting the import quota on Cuba's sugar. Castro in turn nationalized other American properties, as well as many Cuban businesses. On Jan. 3, 1961, U.S. president Dwight Eisenhower broke relations with Cuba.

"Fidel Castro Ruz,"
Encyclopedia of World Biography,
February 7, 2008.

For a league in which more than 30 percent of players are Latino, Selig's unwillingness to move the game despite calls from Latino-community leaders, activists and MLB players spoke volumes about his lack of regard for issues affecting Latinos throughout the country. Rubbing elbows with Castro in 1999, a man he now claims to loathe, speaks even louder.

While Selig has the freedom to do pretty much whatever he damn well pleases, Guillén, who was born in Venezuela and became an American citizen in 2006, apparently doesn't have the right to have unpopular views on Castro.

This isn't Guillén's first dustup over controversial comments about world leaders—or dictators, depending on your perspective. Guillén was lambasted for expressing his admiration for "the man," Venezuelan president Hugo Chávez in a 2006 interview with *Playboy*, after having been criticized for waving the Venezuelan flag and shouting "Viva Chávez!" during the Chicago White Sox's celebration of winning the 2005 World Series. Again Guillén insisted that he was talking about the man, not the politician. What is America coming to if someone born in Venezuela can't speak publicly about the president of Venezuela?

Free Speech

Therein lies the rub. If freedom of speech is truly free, then Guillén has the right to have unpopular views about Castro, Chávez or anyone else for that matter, just as Selig has the right to criticize him for those views.

Baseball is known as America's sport because it was a sport that immigrants from different parts of the world and speaking different languages could embrace. How ironic is it that those whose ancestors came here seeking freedoms—including free speech—now dictate what players and managers of the game can and cannot say, even when those participants are speaking of their own racial, ethnic or national community?

Let me be clear: I think that Guillén is a loudmouth who needs to take it down a thousand decibels. But suspending him for five games for having, and expressing, an opinion on a subject he was asked about is a questionable action—but it proves that my mother is right.

The idea that one has the right to have one's own views about certain matters and to voice those views without fear of retribution is just that—an idea. The reality is that when given a specific platform (the operative word is "given"), people can't assume that they can use that platform to say whatever they think, even when asked.

Words matter, and how those words are sewn together—and how they're communicated, and by whom—matters even more. The ongoing firings of writers, celebrities and media personalities over the written, spoken or digital word serve as a constant reminder that free speech isn't always free—at least not for everyone.

| "Professional sportsmen are singularly ill equipped to deal with or even understand the problems of real life."

Professional Athletes Should Refrain from Expressing Controversial Opinions

Cathal Kelly

Cathal Kelly is a sportswriter for the Toronto Star. *In the following viewpoint, he asserts that professional athletes should not speak out on pressing issues of the day because they are not equipped to do so. Kelly finds that the public puts too much responsibility on athletes to express opinions on matters they are not familiar with and then listens to these opinions as if they have significant meaning—when they obviously do not. The public needs to turn to experts instead of relying on athletes to make moral stands or to clarify complicated political situations, Kelly concludes.*

As you read, consider the following questions:

1. According to Kelly, what did Dieter Graumann say about Germany's soccer team and its visit to Auschwitz?

2. What does Kelly report that the writer Henryk Broder said about Germany's soccer team and its visit to Auschwitz?

3. Who does Kelly believe is a good guy in sports?

In the course of doing this work, you necessarily spend some time in conversation with professional athletes.

Some are decent and some aren't. Some smart, some stupid. Most are pleasantly average in just about every way aside from their physicality and their bank balance. All of them are cagey and the ones who aren't quickly learn to be.

There are few broad strokes that can be used to paint them all, but I'll venture to say this much—I wouldn't want a single one of them speaking on my behalf.

Athletes Make Poor Spokesmen

Professional sportsmen are singularly ill equipped to deal with or even understand the problems of real life.

Every time I watch an athlete tossing his soiled undergarments onto the floor, confident that one of the team's servants will scurry over to pick it up and put it in the hamper the wearer could have aimed for in the first place, I am reminded of this fact.

However, for lack of anyone better to do the job, we've made athletes our de facto diplomats. We want them to weigh in and even lead on the pressing social issues of the day.

We've encouraged them to run for office, despite the fact that their first career is antithetical to the idea of public service. The athletes who go into politics are the worst of the lot—the applause junkies.

We want guys who skipped calculus to lift weights to tell us what to do. There are few greater warnings about the rapid denuding of our intellectual landscape.

A German Controversy

This week [in March 2012], Germany was all in a kerfuffle because someone suggested that the national football team might travel to Poland for this summer's European championships and not visit Auschwitz while there.

Dieter Graumann, head of Germany's Central Council of Jews, said that choosing to skip out on a day trip to the death camp would be "inconceivable."

"By (visiting Auschwitz) they would be showing the whole world that they are prepared to carry a certain amount of responsibility on their shoulders," Graumann said in an interview.

Wrong. Wrong, wrong, wrong. This has nothing to do with Germany, Jews or the Holocaust. This has to do with some 22-year-old mope who has never read a non-illustrated book taking "responsibility" for the German people, or any other sort of people.

"Showing solidarity for dead Jews is a cheap exercise," German Jewish writer Henryk Broder wrote while rubbishing the suggestion. "The people who were murdered can't be killed again, nor can they be rescued retroactively."

That sounds like a pretty good final word.

Cheap Exercises

Speaking of cheap exercises, they sent the [Toronto] Raptors out in camouflage jerseys this past week. Nothing like the sight of an Italian, a Spaniard, a Lithuanian and assorted Americans press-ganged into wearing foreign colours to make you feel extra Canadian. You can talk all day about money raised and good causes, but every business knows that when things aren't going well, the smart move is to wrap yourself in the flag. Whenever I hear anyone in a suit jacket and tie talking about sacrifice and honour, I think of what Dr. [Samuel] Johnson said about patriotism and scoundrels.

Again, this isn't about the troops or Afghanistan or where you fall on the phony left-right political spectrum.

This is about putting an important conversation we rarely seem to have with each other anymore into the hands of a bunch of guys who couldn't care less.

José Calderón [a professional basketball player] is a wonderful person. Really. On the 1-to-10 scale of good guys in sport (where [professional baseball player] A.J. Burnett is a 4 and [professional baseball player] John McDonald is a 9.5), Calderón's an 11.

However, he has no business doing agitprop [political propaganda] on the war effort in prime time, especially if he didn't come up with the idea himself. When I want to know about the war, I'll ask a soldier.

Taking the Blame

This isn't the players' faults. They hate this stuff. This is our fault.

It's our fault that we conflate visibility with wisdom. It's our fault that we've turned on our public institutions and the people who lead them.

It's our fault that we've lost faith in our own ability to reason things out, and instead want a guy who bounces a ball for a living to tell us what to think.

> *"Awareness is not the same thing as tolerance; tolerance still only brings us right up to the edge of what the first openly gay player will experience, and how those around him (peers, fans, corporate leadership) will process it."*

The Free Expression of Athletes Is Curbed When It Interferes with Profits

Bethlehem Shoals

Bethlehem Shoals is the pseudonym of Nathaniel Friedman, a blogger and sports journalist. In the following viewpoint, he points to several recent occasions when professional athletes have been fined or asked to cut out controversial comments because it hurts the team or league's commercial appeal. In a few recent cases, he explains, some controversial comments appear to cater to a specific demographic or political niche group in order to generate branding opportunities and profits. Shoals argues that commerce and free expression are intertwined, and fans should be more astute in recognizing the role both play in modern sports.

As you read, consider the following questions:

1. According to the author, how much was Kobe Bryant fined for using a gay slur on the court?

2. How much was Joakim Noah fined for using the same word?

3. Why was Luke Scott told to cut out his controversial comments, according to Shoals?

As they say on ESPN, May [2011] was huge for the LGBT [lesbian, gay, bisexual, and transgender] community in sports.

(Caveat: When it comes to making gains in sports, generally the term translates to big-money team sports, played by men. Maybe it shouldn't be this way, but those are the games that define and reflect the cultural mainstream.)

Rick Welts, the president and CEO [chief executive officer] of the Phoenix Suns and once the third most powerful man in the league's offices, ended his decades of silence. Suns players Grant Hill and Jared Dudley appeared in a PSA [public service announcement] decrying the casual, trash-talk use of "faggot." The spot, prompted by a Kobe Bryant sideline utterance from April, aired throughout the play-offs. Kobe was fined $100,000, and when [Chicago] Bulls center Joakim Noah used the word in a shouting match with a hostile fan this past month, he was docked $50,000.

More importantly, Noah—raised in a boho [bohemian] household and likely one of the NBA's [National Basketball Association's] most open-minded players—pulled no punches in his apology. It showed how mindlessly even the most liberal of players can throw around a word without even registering his engagement in hate speech.

More High-Profile Support

Suns point guard Steve Nash, the league's go-to lefty, has openly supported gay marriage. Irascible television commentator Charles Barkley, one of the most respected and unfiltered voices in the sport, has been banging that drum for a while now. He went a step further this month, announcing that he didn't think an openly gay NBA player would be all that big a deal.

A lot of this is just talk, or simply acknowledging that words have meaning, even when we don't intend them to. Awareness is not the same thing as tolerance; tolerance still only brings us right up to the edge of what the first openly gay player will experience, and how those around him (peers, fans, corporate leadership) will process it. But there are stirrings, encouraging signs, the social justice equivalent of Mars rover findings. They also pale in comparison to some developments on the other side that, in their marriage of politics and commerce, raise all sorts of new structural concerns.

Hockey may not be as central to the American dialogue as basketball, but there are plenty of teams in this country, and it's a sport on the rise. What's more, since Canada is often a far more progressive place, it makes sense that its national sport might also have something to say about the issue. [New York] Rangers forward Sean Avery, known for his crude, un-PC [politically correct] insults, *Vogue* internship, and unsportsmanlike play, recorded a spot for the New Yorkers for Marriage Equality campaign.

Shortly after it aired, Todd Reynolds, the vice president of Ontario's Uptown Sports [Management] agency, took to Twitter to voice his disapproval. Reynolds tweeted that he was "very sad to read Sean Avery's misguided support of same-gender 'marriage.' Legal or not, it will always be wrong."

True to form, Twitter reacted immediately, prompting more from Reynolds: "To clarify. This is not hatred or bigotry towards gays. It is not intolerance in any way shape or form. I believe we are all equal. . . . But I believe in the sanctity of marriage between one man and one woman. This is my personal viewpoint. I do not hate anyone."

Charles Barkley

Charles Barkley, the talented and controversial star of the Phoenix Suns and later the Houston Rockets, was voted the 1992–93 Most Valuable Player in the National Basketball Association (NBA). For years the outspoken, combative Barkley languished in relative obscurity as his former team, the Philadelphia 76ers, failed to advance in NBA play-off competition. But his inclusion on the 1992 United States Olympic team and his 1992 trade to the Suns provided Barkley with a national audience for both his fabulous basketball talents and his legendary attitude. Eight years later Barkley retired from professional basketball as one of just four NBA stars ever to reach the statistical milestones of twenty thousand points, ten thousand rebounds, and four thousand assists. . . .

In an era when sports superstars found it fashionable to shun the media, Barkley was a sound-bite darling. After any game, win or loss, he could be counted upon to offer opinions on just about everything from his performance to his teammates' abilities to current political events. From time to time his comments caused a tempest, but he rarely apologized or reconsidered anything he said. Barkley was adamant on one point: He did *not* consider himself a role model for youngsters. Political correctness was for government officials, not basketball players, in his opinion. "I believe in expressing what you feel," he told the *New York Times Magazine*. "There are people who hide everything inside—and it's guys like that who kill whole families."

"Charles Barkley,"
Contemporary Black Biography,
July 1, 2008.

It Is Not Personal, It Is Business

Reynolds's "personal viewpoint" excuse doesn't really hold water. Uptown Sports is a small agency, where the line between the personal and the corporate is hard to distinguish. Reynolds told the *National Post* that "that is not the basis on which we run our business. We're not asking questions like that of our clients. And frankly, if Sean Avery were a client of mine, I would support him in his beliefs." Yet Uptown Sports—again, a small agency—has a vice president associated with some very particular, and questionable, positions; its brand name is (now) inseparable from this incident.

Even if Reynolds never intended these tweets as anything more than a statement of personal belief (which, of course, is still problematic), the Uptown Sports brand, for the time being, is a socially conservative one; the players who have stuck with it are at best apolitical and at worst actively embracing the agency's accidental identity. To do so when so many other players had strong reactions against Uptown Sports suggests that this isn't just a fleeting concern. It's on the mind of the sport, and to sit idle is, in effect, taking a stand.

At first blush, this would not appear to be smart business. Agency brands may be less memorable, but athlete brands are obsessed over, and, certainly, players in every sport have at times taken drastic action to "protect the brand." An athlete's brand can have a drastic effect on lucrative opportunities like endorsements and public appearances. And yet Uptown has not lost a single client. It's entirely possible that Uptown, with less to lose and more flexibility than bigger agencies, has made a gamble on appealing to culturally conservative sports fans. If Avery, or an NBA player like Nash, can be perceived as left friendly, why not court the other extreme?

The mechanics of this messaging are especially suspicious. Usually, it's the job of agents to run interference when athletes shoot off their mouths. Here, the agent, rather than playing spin doctor, is saying the thing the athletes can't. And yet, by sticking with Uptown, the pros reap the benefits.

A Clever Businessman?

At least in America, politics are polarizing. The right, religious or otherwise, and to a lesser degree, the left, make for important consumer blocks. Say a Nash or Avery is admired for his stance, aiding his brand. Shouldn't there be other fans out there just clamoring for a player who, however subtly, stands with his values? To be even more cynical about it, maybe Todd Reynolds isn't an incompetent jerk, or an irresponsible one, but a clever strategist. It may be a risky maneuver, but Reynolds serving as mouthpiece makes it less so.

It's no worse for business than Avery's PSA. If anything, there's more of a cushion, more plausible deniability. Forget belief; the Uptown saga could have been nothing more than a publicity stunt in the name of commerce.

If this sounds paranoid, or dystopic, look no further than the Baltimore Orioles' Luke Scott, who has been spouting pro-gun, anti-Obama, birther-esque—at times almost racist—rhetoric for any reporter who cares to listen. The Orioles eventually told Scott, whose act (or rank stupidity) garnered him an ESPN feature, to cut it out in the clubhouse. Note, though, that this order didn't come from Scott's agent or manager, or anyone else with a direct financial stake in his brand. The team doesn't want fans turned off, and turned away from games, by Scott's antics. Anywhere else means more publicity, and of a kind that establishes him firmly as the patron athlete of Tea Party [a conservative political movement] aspirants everywhere.

Finding His Audience

We have a tendency to idealize politics in sports because they appear so rarely, and because explicit statements tend to come from the left. Conservative athletes, by and large, could get away with a few key statements that signaled the whole cluster of values that, by implication, held. What's more, with Muhammad Ali serving as the model, it's inconceivable that they could be intertwined with commerce. At this point, that couldn't be further from the case. Only a true radical like Ali, who was willing to forfeit stardom for his beliefs, transcends branding and moneymaking.

The rise of the radical right, and increased polarization along the lines of issues like gay marriage, changes the calculus. Scott caters to a niche audience the same way that any other identity-driven celebrity does. Let's not kid ourselves: On some level, it will be the same way with the first openly gay NBA or NHL [National Hockey League] player.

> *"Simultaneously loved and hated, [Tim] Tebow drives even those pundits most clueless about sports to argue about his religion, his political beliefs, and the manifestations of them."*

Professional Athletes Should Not Be Criticized for Public Religious Expression

Samuel Coffin

Samuel Coffin is a staff writer for the Harvard Political Review. *In the following viewpoint, he maintains that the widespread mocking of National Football League (NFL) quarterback Tim Tebow is based on the public's discomfort with public displays of religious devotion. Coffin argues that Tebow's very visible public religious expression does not deserve scorn, but the media is at fault for glorifying him as an underdog and generating fan resentment. Coffin also questions whether the media would mock the public religious expression of a player of a different religion, particularly a Muslim or Jewish athlete.*

As you read, consider the following questions:

1. According to the author, what Bible verse did Tim Tebow paint in his eye black in college?

2. What is "Tebowing," according to Coffin?

3. What college quarterback does the author cite as more successful than Tebow on the field?

It does not take a particularly long viewing of ESPN's *Sports-Center* to get more than one's fill of Tim Tebow. Yet, it is simply not the sports media chattering about Tim Tebow; the entire pundit world is now ablaze over the athlete.

Who Is Tim Tebow?

As football fans know, Tim Tebow is currently the starting quarterback of the Denver Broncos. [Editor's note: He was traded to the New York Jets in March 2012 and then signed with the New England Patriots in June 2013]. Before his time in the National Football League (NFL), Tim Tebow played for the Florida Gators, winning two Southeastern Conference championships, two national championships, and the Heisman Trophy. As a quarterback in college, he was highly lauded both for his on-field success and off-field personality. Tim Tebow is a devout evangelical who was known for wearing Bible verses on his eye black. As an NFL quarterback, Tebow hit the national stage this year [2012], leading his team to multiple late comebacks and taking them well into the playoffs.

Tim Tebow, however, has become one of the most polarizing figures in sports. Simultaneously loved and hated, Tebow drives even those pundits most clueless about sports to argue about his religion, his political beliefs, and the manifestations of them. Then, there are those who have grown to hate not necessarily Tim Tebow but the incessant media attention given to him. It is important to note that these two narratives, while linked, are rooted in different aspects. While Tebow should not receive criticism over the expression of his Christian beliefs, the media certainly should be responsible in its portrayal of him.

Tim Tebow

Tim Tebow is an American football player.... After beginning his sports career at [Allen D.] Nease High School in Florida, Tebow attended the University of Florida. He played for four years with the Florida Gators football team, winning numerous awards including the 2007 Heisman Trophy. In 2010 he was drafted to the Denver Broncos as quarterback. He then was traded to the New York Jets [and in 2013 signed with the New England Patriots]. Off the playing field, Tebow is involved in Christian ministry and community service.

"Tim Tebow," Gale Biography in Context, *July 1, 2011.*

Controversy Goes National

In college, Tim Tebow certainly garnered a great deal of media attention, but it was more localized given college football's regional appeal and based generally on his success as a football player. Certainly, his John 3:16 eye black generated some talk, but any non-football praise of him more generally reflected his good character. His debut on the political scene came after his senior season, when Focus on the Family ran an advertisement during the Super Bowl. Pro-choice groups exploded in outrage as word came that Tim Tebow would appear in the pro-life advertisement. Ultimately, the advertisement recalled the situation of his parents, who were approached by physicians advising an abortion of Tim Tebow due to health concerns. The commercial focused on the refusal of Tebow's mother to undergo an abortion, and Tebow himself only makes a brief appearance.

The arguments continued to this year, where the act of "Tebowing" became hot topic. Tim Tebow, after a successful play, often gives a quick prayer on his knee during the game. While it is certainly not inconspicuous, it is nevertheless an expression of his religious belief. Tim Tebow is clearly not thanking God for completing that reception or getting a great block downfield. Rather, it is a note of thanks for the success overall that he has achieved. Yet, "Tebowing" soon became a point of derision, to the point where players sacking Tebow would give their own mock prayer. As the *New York Times*'s sports blog notes, would the media not immediately attack any player mocking the public religious expression of a player of a different religion? Certainly no one would think to criticize a modern-day [professional baseball player] Sandy Koufax for skipping a pennant game because of High Holidays [referring to Jewish holidays].

Religion in Public Life

Rather, it seems today that people are simply unaccustomed to public displays of religious devotion in life. And it is certainly true that a number of other professional athletes, such as [professional baseball player] Albert Pujols, are quite public about their Christian faith. That said, in the ranks of the NFL, the most famous actions of athletes seem to be less than savory. Between Ben Roethlisberger, Michael Vick, and Donté Stallworth, a less publicized but horrific case of a current NFL player who killed a pedestrian while driving drunk, the public isn't particularly used to cases of squeaky-clean athletes. The public in this case is so incredulous at a case such as Tebow's that it almost "has to be" fake. Daniel Foster of *National Review* echoes this feeling and compares it to the major media attention given to preacher scandals. Perhaps there is some dark secret that Tebow is hiding, and the derision of him is based upon the hope of one's existence. However, there is absolutely no indication to believe that Tebow is nothing more than a very fervent Christian who feels it is appropriate to attribute his success to God.

This is not to say that Tebow is beyond reproach. What was mentioned above covers the disdain for Tebow as a public evangelical, and the attacks on his religious expression are inappropriate. However, there is a more legitimate criticism than simply a disagreement with his religious expression: Tebow gets far more attention than he deserves. As a quarterback, he can have moments of brilliance, but fundamentally he has major flaws. His throwing motion looks like he's throwing a shot put, and while his victories are spectacular, his losses are equally embarrassing. Most frustrating for football fans is that he has received much greater love from the sports media than he deserves. In comparing his stats and those of Cam Newton, another mobile quarterback, Newton, a rookie from Auburn, has much more passing yards, touchdowns, and completions than Tebow has had in his two seasons.

Tim Tebow Is Not an Underdog

What is most frustrating is that the media has constructed an image of Tebow as a pitiable underdog. In a commercial for FRS Healthy Energy, Tebow uses lines by his detractors as motivation for his success, such as "They said I couldn't get a D-1 scholarship," "They said I couldn't win a Heisman," and "They said I couldn't win a national championship." The problem is that this hagiography [idolizing biography] as the "underdog" is simply false. According to the major recruiting services, Tim Tebow was a five-star recruit, the highest possible ranking. Both Alabama and Florida, two premier programs in college football, offered Tebow a scholarship. A brief flip through 2008 editions of football previews shows Florida as the clear favorite to win the national championship. Tim Tebow even won the Heisman Trophy as a sophomore in 2007, which was previously unprecedented. To summarize, Tim Tebow was the starting quarterback of one of the best football teams in the best conference in college football. He is many things, but underdog is not one.

Tebow does not deserve scorn, but the media should cool off in its praise of him. This distinction in the criticism of the media treatment, not Tebow himself, must be maintained. It is laudable that there is a good role model for young football fans. Clearly, he should not be criticized for his public expressions of faith. That said, his defenders who want to build him as some eternally persecuted hero against all odds should remember that Tebow was the crusher of underdogs in college. Tebow has gone through a great deal of criticism for his religious beliefs, and clearly that is wrong. However, the media has greatly overreached in trying to build him up as a football underdog struggling against the system.

"The problem here isn't the players' 'faith.' It's the not-so-subtle assumption that every person of faith adheres to the Christian faith—and to a highly traditional version of it, at that."

Professional Athletes Should Not Engage in Excessive Religious Expression

Jonathan Zimmerman

Jonathan Zimmerman is an educator and author. In the following viewpoint, he states that the problem with excessive religious expression in professional sports is that the majority of players come from different faith traditions and do not want to participate in group religious activities. Zimmerman points out that such rituals as the team prayer alienate these other players and threaten team cohesion. He maintains that these group religious rituals only go back a few decades and stemmed from the controversial Supreme Court ruling barring group prayer and Bible readings from public schools.

As you read, consider the following questions:

1. What does the author report that Drew Brees said after the 2010 Super Bowl?

Jonathan Zimmerman, "When Athletes Praise God at the Super Bowl and Other Sports," *Christian Science Monitor*, February 9, 2010. Copyright © 2010 by Jonathan Zimmerman. All rights reserved. Reproduced by permission.

2. According to estimates, what percentage of pro football players are evangelical Christians?

3. What happened to three Muslim football players at New Mexico State University when they decided to pray on their own in 2005?

"God is great."

So said Drew Brees, the most valuable player in last Sunday's Super Bowl [2010], after leading the New Orleans Saints to an upset victory over the Indianapolis Colts.

Such comments have become commonplace on American television, where athletes routinely thank God in postgame prayers and interviews.

Is this a problem? I think it is. And to see why, try to imagine if Brees had made a slightly different statement: "Allah is great."

While some of us might not see anything wrong with that, would network television announcers have applauded Brees as a "man of faith," as he is frequently called?

Would newspapers have published glowing profiles of the other devout members of the Saints, who played up their religious belief during the buildup to the Super Bowl—and thanked God after it?

You already know the answer. The problem here isn't the players' "faith." It's the not-so-subtle assumption that every person of faith adheres to the Christian faith—and to a highly traditional version of it, at that.

They don't, of course. But that's the impression you'd get from watching religious rituals at American sporting events, which inevitably assume a conservative Christian cast.

Tracing the History

Why? The answer lies in the peculiar history of these rituals, which are much more recent than you might guess. For over a century, to be sure, Americans have promoted team sports as vehicles for Christian virtue and character. But loud, demonstrative prayers at athletic events didn't start until the 1960s and '70s, when Christianity faced new challenges from minority faiths.

Most notably, the Supreme Court barred group prayer and Bible reading from the public schools. So conservative Christians devised new ways to bootleg prayers—Christian prayers, of course—into the schools.

The most popular mechanism was the so-called "moment of silence," which 23 states instituted after the Supreme Court rulings. Some school districts replaced their morning prayers with "The Star-Spangled Banner" or "God Bless America," which both invoked God's blessing. Still others began to hold prayers outside normal school hours, especially at—you guessed it—football games.

"We have kicked the Bible out of schools, but coaches realize its importance in the locker room," boasted one minister in St. Petersburg, Florida. Across the state in Miami, site of this year's Super Bowl, players at Miami Senior High School attributed their 1966 national championship to team prayers.

"The Lord Jesus Christ can make a great athlete out of a good one and a winner out of a loser," declared the squad's all-city defensive end. "Wouldn't you rather be a winner than a loser?"

Religious Expression in Professional Sports

The prayer-in-sports ritual would migrate upward over the next decade, from high schools to college and eventually to the pros.

The first NFL [National Football League] player to kneel in prayer after a touchdown—a common sight today—was Philadelphia Eagles running back Herb Lusk, following a 70-yard touchdown run in 1977. Fittingly, Lusk became a minis-

"Tebow Adoration," cartoon by Dave Granlund, www.PoliticalCartoons.com. Copyright © 2012 by Dave Granlund, www.PolicitalCartoons.com.

ter and now serves as the Eagles' team chaplain. Most other NFL teams have chaplains, too, and most of them—like Lusk—are evangelical Christians.

So are an estimated 35 to 40 percent of professional football players. The rest come from other faith traditions, mostly Christian, and they usually don't participate in group prayers. Nor do they make a fuss, which might threaten team cohesion.

But there are exceptions. In 2007, when 30 members of the Detroit Lions started praying after practice—and concluding with a shout, "One, two, three . . . JESUS!"—other players raised their eyebrows. "You can't bring religion up in most workplaces; you can't do a team prayer at the office," explained one player, who didn't participate in the prayer. "So this is something unique that we have to deal with."

He's right. The true victims of sports prayers are in the faith groups that get left out.

What About Other Faiths?

Consider the fate of three Muslim football players at New Mexico State University, where a new coach instituted the Lord's Prayer after practices in 2005. When the Muslims chose to pray on their own, the coach repeatedly asked one of them what he thought of al Qaeda. He eventually dismissed all three Muslims from the team, calling them "troublemakers."

But the real trouble was the prayer, of course, not the players. They sued the university, which settled with them out of court.

I can imagine them, heads bowed after the settlement, saying "Allah is great." But I can't imagine them doing that before a big game, on prime-time TV, while the announcers commend them for their "faith."

Can you?

> *"This instant feedback mechanism is an opportunity for any brand to grow and become more responsive to the market, but it's also threatening, which is why professional sports leagues have adopted policies limiting what athletes say to the public."*

Social Media Can Be Beneficial for Professional Athletes

Lisa Lewis

Lisa Lewis is a journalist and student. In the following viewpoint, she considers the opportunities that social media affords professional athletes and sports programs. Lewis finds that although many athletes have set up their own Twitter accounts and Facebook pages, there is still a lot of experimentation going on to find the best way to engage fans and make money. Social media is beneficial for athletes because it is a way to generate fan interest and fan loyalty, Lewis concludes. She concedes that there are dangers, and athletes must be aware of them in order to take full advantage of social media.

As you read, consider the following questions:

1. Who are Lewis's favorite sports reporters on Twitter?

2. What sports league does Lewis believe has the best fan page?

3. How many followers does Chad Ochocinco have on Twitter, according to Lewis?

Social media is an ever-evolving enigma—everyone now knows that there are tons of opportunities within the online space to make money, gain publicity, and tell the world about oneself, but few people can figure out how to maximize that payoff.

Athletes and sports programs are constantly experimenting with the usefulness of social media. Many pro athletes have their own Twitter streams or Facebook fan pages, but only a few have figured out how to capture the ever-elusive money-maker of social media: fan engagement.

Pros and Cons of Social Media

Once the fans become invested in you, you've created an audience. You've got a captive audience that wants to know what you're doing that's cool and different. It reflects a transnational trend in freedom of information—the economy is becoming more transparent.

However, people are scared to engage fully with their audiences on Twitter, Facebook, and YouTube, because word of mouth is completely organic—if your fans love you or if they hate you, they make it public information. This instant feedback mechanism is an opportunity for any brand to grow and become more responsive to the market, but it's also threatening, which is why professional sports leagues have adopted policies limiting what athletes say to the public.

But be not afraid! For those meek-but-intrigued social media newbies, here are some creative ways in which the Internet is changing the way fans keep up on their favorite sports.

How the Internet Is Changing Sports

1. *Sports reporters on Twitter.* My favorites—ESPN's online columnist Bill Simmons, who is @sportsguy33, and Jay Christensen, the Wiz of Odds, who is at @JayChristensen—cover two opposite ends of the Twitter spectrum. Bill has cultivated an online celebrity persona, interacting frequently with his fans on Twitter and using his feed to pimp his ESPN.com articles on occasion. Simmons is a huge asset to ESPN's online readership because he drives traffic to the site but also serves as an approachable face to the big, national brand name. Jay, on the other hand, uses his Twitter feed much like a micronews aggregator, writing his Reporters' Notebooks features, which summarize relevant collegiate athletics news around the nation, and linking to them from his blog. It's thanks to Jay that I first heard about the rumors of Colorado leaving the Big 12 [college athletic conference]. People like Jay and Bill are keeping the sports media world moving at the speedy pace that social media is taking, and their work helps to make journalism more timely and more relevant.

2. *Interactive Facebook fan pages.* The fan page for the NBA [National Basketball Association], at www.facebook.com/nba, harnesses the viral capabilities of its nearly two million fans by engaging them in asking for feedback every single day. Posting at least two updates per weekday, and more on the weekend, the NBA is constantly adding links to epic slam dunks on YouTube or running polls asking fans about specific players. The coolest thing about this use of a fan page is that it unites fans from every team, offering up content about all the games each week so that there are opportunities for fans from Denver to play nicely with fans from Detroit and for all

fans to weigh in on the best defender in NBA history. In addition, the NBA gets that the best way to have happy fans is to make it worth their while—the Facebook page features giveaways of Xbox consoles as well as opportunities to download cool wallpapers to your iPhone or your BlackBerry. I don't even watch NBA games and I wanted to be a fan—the NBA cares about its community and takes care to deliver quality, useful content to sports fans. No wonder it gets almost two million thumbs-up.

3. *Athletes themselves engaging with fans on Twitter.* The obvious example of this is Mister [Chad] Ochocinco [also known as Chad Johnson] himself, @ogochocinco, who boasts an impressive 773,509 Twitter followers as of press time [in March 2010]. There is absolutely nothing professional about this Twitter feed. There is random usage of capitalization. There are incomplete sentences. Chad does not even make an effort to be politically correct or self-censored in the kinds of things that he posts. Yet, we eat it up—fans love it because it's authentic, real, and not manufactured, sanitized PR [public relations] lingo like so much of the material that professional and collegiate teams put out. If someone else ran his Twitter, would we ever have learned that Ochocinco is an Alvin Ailey [American] Dance [Theater] fan?

Transparency is scary.... Long gone are the days of the private and personal "angry letter." But I see it as progressive—athletic departments can't hide behind desks in their offices, and pro teams can't hide behind managers and owners, making the experience more valuable for the fans. And at the end of the day, isn't that really what sports are all about?

> "*Social media channels offer athletes the opportunity to significantly strengthen their marketability but at the same time—if not handled with care—have the potential to seriously damage their private life, career, athletic performance and 'personal brand.'*"

Social Media Can Be Dangerous for Professional Athletes

Thomas van Schaik

Thomas van Schaik is global brand director at Adidas and contributor to SportsNetworker.com. In the following viewpoint, he asserts that social media sites provide exciting opportunities for professional athletes to engage with fans and offer a glimpse into their personal lives. However, van Schaik cautions, it also has the potential to destroy an athlete's brand and negatively affect their personal lives and careers. There have been several examples of professional athletes posting ill-considered tweets or rants on Facebook, sending explicit e-mails or text messages, or

Thomas van Schaik, "Professional Athletes on Social Media: Why Some Get Fans and Others Fines," *Sports Networker*, September 19, 2011. www.sportsnetworker.com. Copyright © 2011 by Thomas van Schaik. All rights reserved. Reproduced by permission.

leaving raunchy voice mails, van Schaik explains. He concludes that there needs to be more training for pro athletes who are active in social media.

As you read, consider the following questions:

1. What does the author identify as examples of high-profile athletes in "Twitter trouble"?

2. According to the author, what approach is the Ultimate Fighting Championship taking with its athletes and social media?

3. How many followers does Tony Hawk have on Twitter, according to the viewpoint?

Professional athletes can use social media to connect with fans and share their personal lives in ways they never could before. An athlete used to be a number, position, weight class or title. Now, athletes, about whom fans only knew what they read in the papers, have become so much more accessible.

Today even the laggards acknowledge that ignoring social media is no longer an option. Virtually every professional athlete has some kind of social presence. They share who their friends are, their pictures and otherwise offer a view into their personal life like never before. These social media channels offer athletes the opportunity to significantly strengthen their marketability but at the same time—if not handled with care—have the potential to seriously damage their private life, career, athletic performance and "personal brand."

Lessons Learned

As many athletes have found out the hard way, the impact of one ill-considered tweet on an athlete's career can be life-changing. It's like Spiderman said: "*With great power comes great responsibility.*" Lack of consideration or an aggressive rant in a split second of poor judgment can easily result in a (minor or, . . . more often) major incident. It seems ironic that the only way to come to grips with these "modern state-of-the-art communication tools" apparently is through the age-old concept of trial and error.

With . . . @mcuban, @ACromartie, @ItsStephRice, @Ryan Babel, @CV31, @ochocinco, @brianching, @StevieJohnson13, @Cfortson4, and @R_Mendenhall[1] being just a few examples of athletes facing some high-profiled "Twitter trouble."

Others, such as [professional football player] Ray Edwards, [former professional football player] Brett Favre, [professional basketball player] Greg Oden, [professional basketball player] Tony Parker, [professional golfer] Tiger Woods, [Australian cricket player] Shane Warne or, most recently, [former professional boxer] Oscar de la Hoya somehow—naively—assumed their voice mails, pictures or direct "sexting" messages would remain private. The selection above represents only a tiny fraction of the athletes who got themselves in trouble by using a cell phone, PDA [personal digital assistant] or other electronic communications device. All of us know mobile [devices] can—and are—being hacked. It's not that complicated to do. Whether their personal information got hacked, leaked, shared or sold, these athletes will most certainly not be the last to be embarrassed and/or fined because of their (ab)use or underestimation of their mobile device or channel. If you're in the public eye, it's simply better to be safe than sorry.

Freedom of Speech

All athletes are—and should obviously be—free to share their personal ideas and opinions. They should feel encouraged to

---

1. Referring to the Twitter accounts of Mark Cuban, owner of the Dallas Mavericks basketball team; Andre Cromartie, professional football player; Stephanie Rice, Olympic gold medalist; Ryan Babel, Dutch football player; Charlie Villanueva, professional basketball player; Chad Ochocinco, also known as Chad Johnson, professional football player; Brian Ching, professional soccer player; Steve Johnson, professional football player; Courtney Fortson, professional basketball player; and Rashard Mendenhall, professional football player, respectively.

connect with their fans and establish a strong social media profile. Fans want their athletes to be real and "uncensored." Moreover athletes themselves seem to really LOVE Twitter. As pointed out in [a] post on Appinions, many athletes spew cliché after cliché when doing a radio, newspaper or television interview, but once they log onto Twitter it's an opinion free-for-all.

However, as @melinda_travis [Melinda Travis, communications professional] points out in her recent post on the *Sports PR Blog,* many athletes lack the necessary knowledge to turn their social engagement into a success. Others simply tend to forget who their audience is, make spelling errors, use profanity or discuss r-rated subjects. Others allow themselves to be baited or provoked by annoying or opposing fans. Some athletes release their frustrations or anger online without giving ample consideration to the consequences. Frequently athletes lack discretion or assume that their direct messages will remain private. Some athletes still underestimate the importance of their social media channels to their sponsors or believe that because they are engaging their followers in social media this allows them to sidestep traditional media all together. Why would you want to repeat the (expensive) mistakes somebody has already made before you?

What's Wrong with Common Sense?

Many of these considerations apply to you and me, as much as they do to professional athletes. All of us should know what is right or wrong to say. Posting content that will get you in trouble with your boss, colleagues or friends is—generally— not a good way to go. [A] post by @darrenrovell [reporter Darren Rovell] points out "The 100 Twitter Rules to Live By." Darren's post is a great place to start. From there, @Tom Satkowiak [Tom Satkowiak, University of Tennessee associate media relations director] compiled his insightful and really

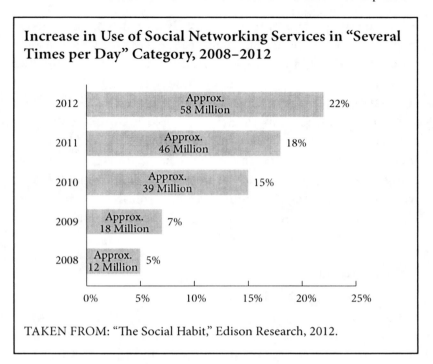

Increase in Use of Social Networking Services in "Several Times per Day" Category, 2008–2012

TAKEN FROM: "The Social Habit," Edison Research, 2012.

helpful "50 Twitter Tips for NCAA Division I Student-Athletes." Well worth a read for athletes at any level!

Many people consider athletes brands. As such, athletes are not only representing themselves, but also their school, team, club, league or sponsor(s). While some of their income is generated by their athletic skills, a lot of their money comes from being a public figure.

Only a few people fake an interest in my tweets but an athlete's words go far beyond the scope of their followers, colleagues, friends and family. It's exactly this public impact that catapults the consequences of an unconsidered tweet into a scandal, potentially damaging the athletes, their organization and their sponsors.

No athlete starts his social media account with the intention of doing anything that could possibly affect his, or another athlete's, performance, like creating the wrong sort of headlines for himself, their team or league. Nevertheless the social media guidelines of the NBA [National Basketball Association], NFL [National Football League], MLB [Major League Baseball], IOC [International Olympic Committee] and the English Professional Footballers' Association (PFA) focus on stipulating everything that is NOT allowed. The Ultimate Fighting Championship [UFC] has taken a completely different approach. This league is actively counseling and coaching their fighters on the use of social media channels and encouraging them to tweet as much as possible. UFC president @dana white [Dana White] (1.5 million Twitter followers) announced that fighters will receive bonuses for adding followers and writing the most creative tweets.

Follow the Leaders

Other athletes are leading by example. Here's . . . the 5 most followed athletes on Twitter: @tonyhawk [professional skateboarder Tony Hawk] with 2,614,278 followers, @lancearmstrong [professional cyclist Lance Armstrong] (3,041,032 followers), @Cristiano [Portuguese footballer Cristiano Ronaldo] (4,021,123 followers), @shaq [professional basketball player Shaquille O'Neal (4,274,104 followers) and @KAKA [Brazilian footballer Ricardo Izecson dos Santos Leite, commonly known as Kaká] (no less than 5,711,014 followers)! These athletes have many people looking at their posts—adding enormous value for their fans, their organization, and their sponsors—and still manage to keep it professional.

Periodical and Internet Sources Bibliography

The following articles have been selected to supplement the diverse views presented in this chapter.

| Josh Alper | "Maryland Politician Asks Ravens to 'Inhibit' Ayanbadejo's Same-Sex Marriage Support," NBC Sports Pro Football Talk, September 6, 2012. http://profootballtalk.nbcsports.com. |

Matt Birk — "NFL's Matt Birk: Let's Protect Marriage—and Speech," *Minnesota Star-Tribune*, October 2, 2012.

Elizabeth DiNovella — "In Defense of Ozzie Guillen," *Progressive*, April 11, 2012.

Lisa Fabrizio — "Tebowphobia," *American Spectator*, December 14, 2011.

Jamilah King — "Are Sports Champions Obligated to Score Political Points, Too?," ColorLines.com, June 6, 2011.

Charles P. Pierce — "Tebow's Religion: Fair Game," Grantland.com, December 19, 2011.

Teresa Puente — "Marlins Suspend Ozzie Guillen over Castro Comments but They Should Have Fired Him," *Chicago Now*, April 10, 2012.

Michelangelo Signorile — "Brendon Ayanbadejo, Baltimore Ravens Linebacker, Talks Gay Marriage and LGBT Rights," *Huffington Post*, September 12, 2012.

Jay Scott Smith — "Pro Athletes Take Rare Stand in Trayvon Martin Response," TheGrio.com, March 27, 2012.

Paul Whitefield — "C'mon, Ozzie Guillen's a Baseball Manager, Not a Diplomat," *Los Angeles Times*, April 10, 2012.

OPPOSING
VIEWPOINTS®
SERIES

CHAPTER 4

What Are Some Controversies Surrounding Professional Athletes?

Chapter Preface

The story of former National Football League (NFL) running back Jamal Lewis proves to be a cautionary tale for aspiring professional athletes. During his career, Lewis had a series of impressive accomplishments on the field. He was a 2003 Pro Bowl selection, a 2003 All-Pro player, and was a member of the Baltimore Ravens team that won the Super Bowl in 2001. Over his career, he ran for more than ten thousand yards and had fifty-eight rushing touchdowns. A nagging knee injury led Lewis to retire at the age of thirty-two in 2009 after nine seasons in the NFL.

Like all elite professional football players, Lewis was well compensated for his work, earning tens of millions of dollars. Early in his career, he signed a six-year, $35.3 million contract with the Ravens, and in 2006 signed another million-dollar contract that made him the highest paid running back in the NFL that year.

Lewis put all that money to work, investing in real estate ventures, theme parks, and resorts, as well as a cross-country trucking business that had a fleet of two hundred trucks. He began to take out loans for his businesses and investments that could not be repaid. The economic downturn negatively affected many of his investments. He bought multiple homes and reportedly lived a lavish lifestyle. In April 2012, Lewis filed for bankruptcy.

Jamal Lewis is only one of a number of athletes who have suffered financial bankruptcy after their lucrative careers. Other high-profile professional athletes who have also experienced financial difficulties include former NFL superstars Warren Sapp and Lawrence Taylor, former boxer Mike Tyson, former National Basketball Association (NBA) stars Kenny Anderson and Allen Iverson, golfer John Daly, and soccer legend Diego Maradona.

In fact, stories like Lewis's are common. Annamaria Lusardi, a George Washington University School of Business professor, observes that athletes have challenges when it comes to money management. "These are talented people, but with very little expertise in financial matters," she states in a 2012 article in the *Baltimore Sun*. "You take a 20-year-old, and give them millions of dollars. Often there is very little guidance given to them. And this is a very risky career. Their careers can end when they are very young because of injuries."

Lusardi offers workshops for professional athletes to provide sound financial guidance. In recent years, there have been more and more resources for athletes looking to better understand financial matters and to formulate a long-term and successful strategy for their wealth.

Financial education is one of the subjects examined in the following chapter, which focuses on recent controversies surrounding professional athletes. Other viewpoints in the chapter explore gambling, salaries, and whether athletes receive preferential treatment when accused of a crime.

> *"It is time for college and professional sports to outline and execute a real program to help players who might have a gambling problem."*

Gambling Is a Problem for Professional Athletes

Arnie Wexler

In the following viewpoint, Arnie Wexler maintains that gambling is a problem for professional athletes because the same characteristics that make them elite athletes—competitive personalities, high levels of energy, distorted optimism—also make them vulnerable to developing a gambling addiction. Wexler finds that professional sports organizations do not want to admit that there is a problem with gambling addiction and have therefore been slow to address it. These organizations, Wexler declares, must design and implement programs to help players deal with their gambling addictions. Arnie Wexler is a writer; a certified compulsive gambling counselor; and codirector of Arnie and Sheila Wexler Associates, a firm that trains compulsive gambling counselors. Arnie and Sheila Wexler have provided extensive training on Compulsive, Problem, and Underage Gambling, to more than 40,000 gaming employees (personnel and executives) and have written Responsible Gaming Programs for major gaming companies. In addition, they have worked with Gaming Boards and Regulators, presented educational workshops nationally and internationally, and have provided expert witness testimony. Sheila Wexler is the Executive Director of the Compulsive Gambling Foundation. They also run a national help line (888 LAST BET) and work at Recovery Road, a treatment facility in Palm Beach Gardens, Florida, that specializes in the treatment of those suffering with gambling addiction.

As you read, consider the following questions:

1. According to the National Gambling Impact Study Commission, how many compulsive gamblers are there in the United States?

2. How many Americans are at risk of becoming compulsive gamblers, according to the National Gambling Impact Study Commission cited by Wexler?

3. What key manual does the author cite as recognizing compulsive gambling, alcoholism, and chemical dependency as addictions?

In May 1996, Horace Balmer, the NBA's [National Basketball Association's] vice president for security, had two speakers flown to Norfolk, Va., whose messages were very disturbing. The two speakers were Michael Franzese, a former mob boss who fixed professional and college games for organized crime, and Arnie Wexler, who for 23 years was a compulsive gambler. Franzese said, "I talked to the NBA rookies earlier this season and it's amazing how many confided to me that they have gambling habits. I'm not going to mention their names, but if I did, you would know them. I personally got involved in compromising games with players, and it all came through their gambling habits."

Assessing the Problem

Twelve years ago, as a compulsive gamblers counselor, I was asked to fly to New York to the NBA office in Manhattan to meet with league officials, players, and union officials concerned about players' gambling. I was told, "We have a problem, and we're trying to find out how bad the problem is." Officials asked me to keep my calendar open for the spring of the following year and told me they wanted me to address every team and player in the league. They then flew my wife in, and we had a second meeting. They asked us to develop questions that were going to be given to the players to answer. "We need to know how big the gambling problem is in the NBA," they said.

When I hadn't heard from the NBA, I called and asked, "When do we start?" The talks were cancelled, and the response I got was this: "They said that the higher-ups didn't want the media to find out."

Some years ago, I was on a TV show with Howard Cosell (*ABC SportsBeat*). The topic was "Does the Media Encourage the Public to Gamble?" NBA commissioner David Stern said: "We don't want the week's grocery money to be bet on the outcome of a particular sporting event." Yet on Dec. 11, 2009, commissioner David Stern told SI.com (the website for *Sports Illustrated*) that legalized gambling on the NBA "may be a huge opportunity." I wonder how many addicted gamblers placed the first bet they ever made on an NBA game? The National Gambling [Impact] Study Commission said that there are "5 million compulsive gamblers and 15 million at risk in the U.S." Forty-eight percent of the people who gamble bet on sports.

An Authoritative Voice

Get the real scoop: Talk to me, Arnie Wexler, one of the nation's leading experts on the subject of compulsive gambling and a recovering compulsive gambler. I placed my last

Gambling in the United States

In 1984, all forms of gambling (casinos, lotteries, pari-mutuel betting: the three segments of the gambling industry) accounted for less than $15 billion in revenues. In 1995, these gambling activities generated $55.3 billion in revenues, nearly a 400 per cent increase in 11 years. Gambling had become the largest component of the American entertainment industry. It had also become a means of salvation in terms of economic development for troubled urban areas ranging from Chicago to New Bedford, Massachusetts. But the multiple roles that gambling presently fulfils, namely a form of entertainment, a method of raising revenue for states and a measure that would provide economic relief for depressed areas, are hardly unique in American history.

Richard A. McGowan,
"A Short History of Gambling in the United States,"
Government and the Transformation of the Gaming Industry.
Cheltenham, UK: Edward Elgar, 2001.

bet on April 10, 1968, and have been involved in helping compulsive gamblers ever since for the last 40 years. Through the years, I have spoken to more compulsive gamblers than anyone else in America and have been fighting the injustice of how sports, society and the judicial system deal with compulsive gamblers.

Athletes may be more vulnerable than the general population when you look at the soft signs of compulsive gambling: high levels of energy, unreasonable expectations of winning, very competitive personalities, distorted optimism, and bright with high IQs. It is time for college and professional sports to outline and execute a real program to help players who might have a gambling problem. Yet college and professional sports still do not want to deal with this. They do not want the media and public to think there is a problem.

There Is a Problem

Over the years, I have spoken to many college and professional athletes who had a gambling problem. One NCAA [National Collegiate Athletic Association] study a few years ago reported: "There is a disturbing trend of gambling among athletes in college." You can't think that these people will get into the pros and then just stop gambling. Compulsive gambling is an addiction just like alcoholism and chemical dependency, and all three diseases are recognized by the American Psychiatric Association's diagnostic and statistical manual. Nevertheless, we treat compulsive gambling differently than the other addictions. Society and professional sports treat people with chemical dependency and alcoholism as sick persons—send them to treatment and get them back to work. Sports looks at compulsive gamblers as bad people and bars them from playing in professional sports. There are people in various sports halls of fame who are convicted drug addicts and alcoholics, yet compulsive gamblers are unable to get into these halls of fame. In fact, as far as professional sports goes, an alcoholic and chemical-dependent person can get multiple chances, whereas a gambler cannot.

If colleges and professional leagues wanted to help the players, they would run real programs that seriously address the issue of gambling and compulsive gambling. Education and early detection can make a difference between life and death for some people who have or will end up with a gambling addiction. One sports insider said to me: "Teams need to have a real program for players, coaches and referees, and they need to let somebody else run it. When you do it in-house, it's like the fox running the chicken coop. You must be kidding yourself if you think any player, coach or referee is going to call the league and say, 'I've got a gambling problem, and I need help.'"

> "Woe to the pro athlete who is even considered to be in the company of gamblers."

Gambling Is Not a Problem for Professional Athletes

Brad Parks

Brad Parks is an author and journalist. In the following viewpoint, he decries the hysteria surrounding professional sports and gambling, arguing that it is an irrelevant concern in the modern age. Players make such large sums of money in the modern era, Parks contends, that it is highly unlikely that they would be influenced or pressured by gamblers to throw games or shave points. Parks points to the hypocrisy of professional sports leagues and their warnings to players regarding gambling when a variety of professional teams and leagues license their brands to state and regional lotteries.

As you read, consider the following questions:

1. What year did the infamous Chicago Black Sox scandal occur, according to the viewpoint?

2. According to the author, who was the NBA's last alleged fixer?

3. When does the author say that the last surviving member of the Black Sox passed away?

As a former sportswriter turned crime fiction author, I've long been attuned to the broad intersection between our games and our legal improprieties.

Some of my earliest visits to courtrooms and police precincts came as I chased stories involving one malfeasant athlete or another. There were times in my newspaper career when I thought they should merge the sports section with the police report, strictly as a matter of efficiency.

But there's always been one aspect of crime and sports that never made much sense to me: The hysteria surrounding pro sports and gambling.

An Outdated Crime

Seriously. The last known fix of a professional baseball game involved the infamous White Sox—aka the Black Sox—and it occurred in 1919, a year after the end of the First World War and a year before women got the right to vote.

The NFL [National Football League] hasn't had a fixing scandal since 1946, when the immortal—or perhaps not so immortal—Frank Filchock and Merle Hapes were questioned shortly before the championship game.

The NBA's [National Basketball Association's] last alleged fixer was Jack Molinas, who was banned from the league in 1954 for betting on games involving his own team, the Fort Wayne Pistons.

What do these have in common? They're at least half a century in our rearview mirror, they involve athletes who are now long dead, and they took place at a time when the average professional athlete wasn't paid much better than the average plumber.

Times Have Changed

The economics of sports have changed dramatically since that time, to the point where it doesn't make a shred of sense for a pro jock to be tempted by the penny-ante bribes of a game-fixer. The minimum salaries in all the major professional sports leagues are in the hundreds of thousands of dollars. The average salaries are in the millions of dollars.

Not even the mob can compete with those kinds of wages.

And yet, every few years, there seems to be another hullabaloo about athletes and their betting habits. Lots of people got in a snit over [professional basketball player] Michael Jordan's gambling, as if he didn't have plenty of dough to blow on an innocent half-million-dollar wager or two. [Former professional hockey player and head coach] Wayne Gretzky's otherwise unsullied reputation got a tarnishing a few years back when he was indirectly implicated—though never formally charged—in a gambling ring involving one of his assistant coaches. And, of course, it's well known that if [former professional baseball player and manager] Pete Rose had "merely" beat his wife, snorted cocaine or kicked homeless people for fun, he'd be in the Hall of Fame by now.

Instead, Rose bet on baseball, the most mortal of all the sporting sins. And because of it, he has been banned from baseball for the last 22 years, which is almost as long as he played it.

Gambling Hysteria

Woe to the pro athlete who is even considered to be in the company of gamblers. All of the major professional sports leagues have handsomely paid security staffs, chock-full of former high-level law enforcement officials, who monitor their players' activities in this area. Every league has, as part of its rookie orientation, stern warnings about the evils of associating with gamblers.

It is a paranoia layered with both absurdity and hypocrisy.

The 1919 Black Sox Scandal

Often dubbed the greatest scandal in sports history, the "Black Sox" story is one of how greed and deception came to rule the diamonds during the 1919 World Series. The Chicago White Sox, a team consisting of some of the greatest players the game had ever known—men like "Shoeless" Joe Jackson and George "Buck" Weaver—seemed a lock to take home the trophy. When they lost, and when it was later revealed that eight men on the team had agreed to "fix" the series for gamblers, the series of events that followed would tarnish the nation's pastime in the public eye. It would also ruin the careers of the players involved, and the 1919 Chicago White Sox would become known to baseball fans everywhere, forever, as the Chicago "Black" Sox.

"1919 Chicago White Sox," Gale U.S. History in Context, *2012.*

Because, on the one hand, the leagues are saying, sternly, don't bet on anything. On the other hand, a variety of pro teams and leagues make money licensing themselves to state and regional lotteries (a form of gambling). Major League Baseball and the NBA . . . have both eyed placing franchises in Las Vegas, the nation's wagering capital and also its last large untapped pro sports market. For that matter, the WNBA [Women's National Basketball Association] has had a team, the Connecticut Sun, playing in the Mohegan Sun casino since 2003.

Facing Reality

Now, granted, college sports are a different ball game. The kids playing them are often dirt poor and, more to the point, they're kids: by definition, prone to stupidity. And every few years or so, the NCAA [National Collegiate Athletic Association] weathers a point-shaving scandal, particularly in college basketball, where as one of five players on the floor, a single athlete can make a sizable difference in a game's outcome.

But when it comes to pro sports and betting? It's time to get real.

Instead, what we get is the spectacle like what happened in New Jersey a few years back, where a state assemblyman was pushing for legalized sports betting in Atlantic City. A lawyer for the NFL [National Football League] testified before the assembly about the "serious problems for team sports" that arise from gambling. He cited, as an example, the 1919 Black Sox scandal.

The last surviving member of the Black Sox, Swede Risberg, died in 1975. The paranoia his infamous team helped create should have been allowed to die with him.

> "The [National Football League] conducts workshops for rookies covering topics such as substance abuse, sex education, gambling, domestic violence and personal finance, but their effectiveness is a matter for debate."

Professional Athletes Need Better Financial Education

Russ Wiles

Russ Wiles is a sports journalist. In the following viewpoint, he discusses the shocking trend of professional athletes who encounter bankruptcy or severe financial problems shortly after retiring from professional competition. Wiles reveals that there are a number of factors that contribute to the problem, including a sense of entitlement, reckless spending, and poor financial advice. Professional athletes need to take control of their own financial education to avoid many of the pitfalls that affect others, Wiles concludes.

As you read, consider the following questions:

1. According to 2009 *Sports Illustrated* estimates cited by Wiles, what percentage of NFL players are bankrupt or facing serious financial stress within two years of ending their playing careers?

2. According to those same 2009 estimates, what percentage of NBA players are broke within five years of retiring from pro basketball?

3. How long is the average professional football career, according to the NFL Players Association, as cited in the viewpoint?

More than 200 college students will get a chance to become instant millionaires when the NFL [National Football League] holds its draft this week [in April 2012].

But fast-forward 20, 10 or just five years down the road, and many of this year's crop of NFL rookies, like players before them, could end up broke.

The financial rise and fall of professional athletes is one of those perplexing things that the other 99 percent just can't understand: How can anyone blow through at least several hundred thousand dollars, and perhaps tens of millions of dollars, in a few years? Yet many pro athletes have done just that. You could compile an all-star team of players who wound up bankrupt or in financial distress.

A Hazard of the Trade?

Though financial woes can beset all sorts of athletes—skater Dorothy Hamill, baseball players Lenny Dykstra and Jack Clark, boxer Mike Tyson, pro golfer John Daly come to mind—the condition seems acute among basketball and football stars.

Sports Illustrated estimated in 2009 that 78 percent of NFL players are bankrupt or facing serious financial stress within two years of ending their playing careers and that 60 percent of NBA [National Basketball Association] players are broke within five years of retiring from the game. A starting lineup of financial-distress examples could include Terrell Owens, Lawrence Taylor, Michael Vick, Deuce McAllister and Bernie Kosar in football, and Allen Iverson, Scottie Pippen, Latrell Sprewell and Antoine Walker in basketball.

The factors contributing to financial ruin are numerous. Most people receiving a sudden windfall would be tempted to spend a good chunk of it quickly. This tendency might be pronounced when there's a sense of entitlement—these are star athletes who have heard how great they are all their lives, after all.

"When a 21-year-old kid gets such big numbers, they go out and buy the big house and the fancy car," said Robert Luna of SureVest Capital Management in Phoenix and the financial adviser to Arizona Cardinals offensive lineman Levi Brown. "Before they know it, they're out of the league and their income drops significantly."

Then there are the legions of hangers-on who flock to the rich and famous.

"All sorts of people and advisers started calling," said Brown, recalling what happened to him after being selected as the fifth overall pick in the 2007 NFL draft. "In any business where you make a lot of money, there are people trying to get their hands on it."

Not Living Within Means

It's not just cars and houses, though. The big bucks also give athletes an opportunity to indulge in all sorts of passions, hobbies and ill-advised behaviors that can generate financial consequences later, from baseball slugger Jack Clark's extensive rare-car collection to NBA star Iverson's $860,000 tab for unpaid jewelry, interest, court costs and legal fees in a dispute with an Atlanta jewelry store.

Gambling and alcohol and drug addictions have been linked to money problems for others. So, too, have marriages and affairs that lead to child-support and alimony payments. An attorney representing Dennis Rodman recently told a judge that Rodman no longer could make child- and spousal-support payments, though the former NBA defensive star initially denied being broke.

The NFL conducts workshops for rookies covering topics such as substance abuse, sex education, gambling, domestic violence and personal finance, but their effectiveness is a matter for debate.

"They try to give you some background, and it's better than nothing," Brown said. "At least you know the statistics for what's ahead."

Many pro athletes may assume the money will keep flowing in for years, but that's usually not the case. The average pro football career is only 3 and one-half years, according to the NFL Players Association, and a lot of the money that makes the contract-signing headlines will never be paid.

"They could have cut him in the first year," said Luna, referring to Brown. "He could have collected very little."

In fact, Brown was cut by the Cardinals earlier this year [in 2012], though he was re-signed by the team a few days later to a five-year, $30 million contract, of which $8 million is guaranteed.

Even athletes who play professionally for many years will eventually need to downsize their finances. That makes them different from most workers, who generally can anticipate higher earnings over time.

"Unlike a young physician who will be making a lot more money 10, 20 or 30 years down the road, an athlete like Levi is getting it all up front," Luna said.

The Wrong People

Athletes also are susceptible to hooking up with the wrong advisers and trusting them implicitly.

"Often, it's a high school or college friend or somebody they knew early in their careers," said Richard Dozer, former president of the Arizona Diamondbacks who now serves as chairman of the Phoenix branch of GenSpring Family Offices, which includes some pro athletes as clients. "It's family and friends a large percentage of the time."

Many athletes act on referrals, sometimes from teammates, that turn out to be toxic. News reports indicate that several members of the Denver Broncos lost perhaps $20 million combined through a scam, linked to a hedge-fund manager, in which players referred one another before the deal blew up.

"A player hears that his teammate has gotten great returns, so he wants to go with that guy, too," Dozer said.

Brown, the Cardinals lineman, relies on a team of advisers that includes an estate-planning attorney, an insurance expert and a certified public accountant.

"We're all independent advisers, so there are checks and balances," Luna said.

He noted that major scams, such as the one perpetrated by Bernie Madoff and which included Hall of Fame pitcher Sandy Koufax as an investor, could have been avoided or minimized with a separation of oversight and third-party custody of assets.

Many financial problems also can be skirted by exercising a healthy dose of skepticism.

Athletes should be grilling prospective advisers about their fees and asking what could go wrong with an investment.

"If someone is promising 25 percent annual returns for several years, ask yourself why everyone isn't doing this," Dozer said.

Although athletes may not want to reveal their lack of sophistication, it's important that they spend time interviewing prospective advisers and asking questions, even dumb ones. Do that enough, Dozer said, and they'll start to spot red flags.

Boring Is Good

Low financial literacy makes many athletes susceptible to getting scammed or suffering losses in high-risk investments. Young adults in general aren't experienced with money and often don't have good role models as savers, homeowners or investors.

Low financial literacy shows up in a poor understanding of how investments work, what constitutes realistic returns and reasonable fees, and how advisers are supposed to interact with clients. Athletes often delegate too much and oversee too little. Some entrust others not just to make the big financial moves but to pay routine bills.

Many athletes also gravitate toward tangible, glitzy business ventures such as restaurants, car dealerships, motion pictures or stakes in new inventions. Perhaps because they're accustomed to life in the fast lane, they often don't seem interested in passive and arguably boring investments such as stocks or bonds.

"It's a little more sexy to have a restaurant in downtown Scottsdale than a muni-bond fund," Luna said.

Risky Investments

But restaurants and other business ventures frequently carry an elevated potential for failure and may require a time commitment that the athlete lacks. When a sports star's finances blow up, it's almost never because the player had too much invested in a stock-market index fund or a portfolio of municipal bonds.

Brown admits making a bad investment in a restaurant that failed. But he mainly holds stocks, bonds, mutual funds and other fairly mundane investments. He also said he takes personal interest in his portfolio, shares in financial decisions with his wife, Lynnette, and doesn't live beyond his means.

"The budget is the first step in figuring this out," Brown said, adding that his biggest financial fear is returning to his childhood lifestyle in Norfolk, Va., where his father served as a Marine. Although he credits his parents for doing well with what they had, he said the family at times lived paycheck to paycheck.

Brown also is working on a master's degree in industrial and labor relations at Pennsylvania State University, where he played football. While many pro athletes attend college, they don't all graduate, and lacking a degree can make the eventual transition back to mainstream life more difficult.

But a college education doesn't guarantee financial success. For athletes and others, some vital money lessons are learned the hard way.

> *"Professional athletes are among our most pampered souls, having been indulged from prepubescence by doting parents, coaches and agents who see their talent as an eventual lottery ticket to riches."*

Professional Athletes Are Overpaid

Dan K. Thomasson

Dan K. Thomasson is a former editor of the Scripps Howard News Service. In the following viewpoint, he reflects on the days when athletes did not make much money but played for the love of the game. Thomasson argues that today's athletes make a lot of money but are pampered, unprofessional, and selfish. In addition, he maintains, they have been infected with a sense of entitlement that leads to other bad behaviors. Thomasson concludes that these modern athletes are a result of a bad system: overindulgent parents, money-grubbing agents, permissive coaches, and fans who care only about winning.

As you read, consider the following questions:

1. For what team does Albert Haynesworth play, according to the viewpoint?

2. According to the author, for how much did the late John Wooden play professional basketball?

3. How much does the author say that Haynesworth's contract was worth?

After enduring months of stultifying debate over a reluctant, divisive and petulant defensive lineman who was paid millions of dollars but showed little or no interest in playing, thoughts naturally turn back to those days when only a handful of professional athletes made not much more than a living wage but participated for the love of the game. It hasn't been that long ago.

The mistakes made in the hiring and handling of Albert Haynesworth, a 300-pound-plus behemoth, admittedly talented tackle when he wanted to play, are numerous. Not the least of these was his seeming refusal to perform under the letter or spirit of his contract and the club's failure to perform due diligence on his character before signing him. He will now appeal a suspension without pay despite overwhelming evidence of intransigence.

How important is this? Not very, except to the legion of loyal Washington Redskins fans, particularly the regular ticket holders, who have been cheated and exploited for years now by an owner who obviously wouldn't know a football from a softball, but has made untold millions off them.

Daniel Snyder [the owner of the Washington Redskins] is a kid who got rich on someone else's money and thought how great it would be to be a "sportsman" who could associate with and decide the fate of guys he was never big enough to join on the playing field.

Professionalism in America

What makes this worth discussing is what it says about the state of professionalism in America. Teachers who don't want to teach. Doctors who don't want to doctor. It is a metaphor

Sports Salaries Worldwide, 2012

Rank	Team	League	Average Annual Pay $
12	San Antonio Spurs	NBA	$5,450,135
11	Manchester United	EPL	$5,521,423
10	Internazionale	Serie A	$5,700,915
9	Philadelphia Phillies	MLB	$5,817,965
8	Bayern Munich	Bundesliga	$5,907,652
7	Milan	Serie A	$6,104,769
6	New York Yankees	MLB	$6,186,322
5	LA Lakers	NBA	$6,278,088
4	Chelsea	EPL	$6,795,899
3	Manchester City	EPL	$7,403,754
2	Real Madrid	La Liga	$7,796,637
1	Barcelona	La Liga	$8,680,569

TAKEN FROM: "Global Sports Salaries Survey 2012,"
Sportingintelligence.com, May 2, 2012.

for the excesses in entertainment that keep tens of millions of devoted fans glued to their TV sets and the comparative few who can afford the exorbitant prices to be in the arenas. Professional athletes are among our most pampered souls, having been indulged from prepubescence by doting parents, coaches and agents who see their talent as an eventual lottery ticket to riches. Along the way it is no wonder they develop a sense of entitlement that frequently leads them into terrible practices.

This tarnished system produces far too many Haynesworths in the rarefied atmosphere of collegiate and professional athletics. While it always has existed to some degree, it took on new dimensions with the huge cash flow of television. A very good friend, the late Dr. Kenneth Haggerty, who was an all-star in New York City prep basketball and later after World War II a captain of the Holy Cross basketball team that included Bob Cousy, explained once that he had been recruited by the Boston Celtics but turned them down because the pay was only $3,000 a year. It was a paltry sum, he said, compared to the amount he expected to earn as an oral surgeon. Do you know a dentist today that makes an average NBA [National Basketball Association] player's pay?

The brilliant American painter, Wilson Hurley, whose art brings six and seven figures, put it this way: "I'm getting so I can just about match the salary of a good outfielder." The late, great John Wooden played professional basketball for $5 a game.

Albert Haynesworth

When he signed with the Redskins, Haynesworth's contract was estimated at more than $100 million if played out. About $41 million was coach Mike Shanahan's efforts to rebuild what is now a third-rate franchise except in profits. For that amount, he clearly considered himself immune from the same responsibilities as his teammates and his coaches.

It would be wrong to tar with the same brush all those who play some kind of professional team sport. A large number are outstanding men and women who aren't tainted by the mountains of cash thrust upon them and who take their obligations seriously. Unfortunately, however, too many regard themselves as special.

Who's to blame? To quote the late, great possum phenomenon Pogo, "We have met the enemy and he is us."

"There should not be a double standard for star athletes, entertainers, or politicians who are hired as soon as their debt to society has been paid and regular citizens who still can contribute to society but have no fame or special skills."

Professional Athletes Who Commit Crimes Receive Preferential Treatment

RMuse

RMuse is an opinion columnist and blogger. In the following viewpoint, RMuse scrutinizes the case of Michael Vick, a professional football player who was incarcerated for running a dogfighting operation. Unlike many other ex-convicts in his position, RMuse explains, Vick will be given another chance and will be making millions of dollars playing quarterback in the National Football League (NFL). This, RMuse argues, exposes the double standard for athletes, entertainers, and politicians when it comes to receiving preferential treatment. The justice system is unequal and favors those with money and fame, according to the author.

As you read, consider the following questions:

1. What did Tucker Carlson say should happen to Michael Vick, according to the author?

2. According to the US Department of Justice as cited by RMuse, how many Americans are incarcerated?

3. What is the cost of incarcerating the American prison population, according to the US Department of Justice as cited by the author?

There is an uproar and outrage over President [Barack] Obama's comments to Philadelphia Eagles owner Jeff Lurie regarding the [football] team giving Michael Vick a second chance after he completed his federal prison sentence for running a dogfighting ring. Criticism has come from animal rights activists and political pundits who never miss a chance to criticize the president regardless of the subject or issue being discussed.

Tucker Carlson, a substitute political commentator for Fox News, went so far as to say Vick should have been executed for his involvement in dogfighting. Carlson is a fervent animal rights activist, but certainly doesn't understand the nature of the law. There is no question that for animal lovers, Vick's crimes were as hideous as is possible, but the law does not recommend the death penalty for Vick's crime. The Eagles' quarterback served his time and paid his debt to society, so calls for execution are extreme and contrary to the tenets of America's criminal justice system.

A Second Chance

The question though is not whether Vick deserves execution, but whether he deserved a second chance after serving his sentence. President Obama condemned Vick for his crimes, but was right in being grateful for Vick's second chance to become a productive citizen. The primary purpose of Obama's call to Lurie was to discuss and praise the Eagles organization for installing wind turbines in an effort to promote green energy.

Many Americans do not think it is appropriate that Vick was given a second chance and it reflects a long-standing belief that convicted felons are not worthy of the same rights as all Americans. A valid question is would Vick have been given a second chance if he wasn't a star athlete? The answer is most certainly "no" based on hiring practices across the country, and it is especially true now that employers can easily make background checks on applicants in a matter of minutes. Unfortunately, employers will find more of their applicants have a criminal history because such a large number of Americans are either in the penal system or are ex-convicts.

America imprisons more people than any country on earth, and as the ex-convicts reenter society they find it increasingly difficult to find employment because of their convictions. Based on statistics from the [US] Department of Justice, the number of Americans incarcerated, on parole, or on probation is one in every thirty-one adults, or about 7.3 million Americans. The greatest percentages of arrests were for consensual (victimless) crimes. Victimless crimes are currently illegal activities that result in no harm or damage to another person or individual's property and include such activities as recreational drug use, gambling, prostitution, pornography, drunk driving, and traffic violations. Juvenile crimes are not included in the 7.3 million figure and make up less than 5% of the overall corrections system population.

If those figures are not alarming, consider that 1 in every 45 Americans is on parole or probation and of that figure, the number of star athletes on parole or probation is infinitesimal. For convicted felons who have served their time like Michael Vick, their chances of finding any employment are increasingly slim and it explains why the recidivism rate is so high among ex-convicts; that is exactly what the prison industry wants. The cost of incarcerating the prison population in America is in excess of $68 billion annually, and it explains why unions representing corrections officers wield such power and influence over legislatures in every state in the Union. In a state like California, the cost to house and maintain the prison population far exceeds the education budget, and it explains why there is a push to privatize the prison system. It also explains why lobbyists pressure legislators to vote against bills that would offer education and rehabilitation to parolees so they can find gainful employment once they are out of the corrections system.

The way the system works now, a parolee without an education or adequate counseling will be back in prison within 1 to 3 years because they cannot find employers willing to give them a second chance. Employers like Walmart or McDonald's will not hire ex-convicts and one has to wonder if there is collusion with the prison industry to keep felons in the system.

The Double Standard

Perhaps President Obama is setting a precedent by thanking Lurie for giving Michael Vick a second chance at being a productive citizen. With so many Americans in the corrections system for victimless crimes, there is a need for reform to delineate between dangerous criminals and those who harm no one. There should not be a double standard for star athletes, entertainers, or politicians who are hired as soon as their debt to society has been paid and regular citizens who still can contribute to society but have no fame or special skills.

The man who was caught with a prostitute should have the same opportunity as the man who killed dogs because they didn't perform, but that is not the case. There is no equity in the system as it stands, and the way it works now the person who is not famous is most likely going to end up back in prison because they have no prospects for employment or the chance to contribute to society.

The Case of Michael Vick

One of the most gifted athletes in the National Football League (NFL), Michael Vick was a superstar quarterback for the Atlanta Falcons from 2001 to 2006. He was the NFL's highest-paid player and a perpetual presence on highlight reels, but his play was as inconsistent as it was spectacular. Then in 2007 his career was abruptly derailed when it emerged that he had for many years operated an illegal and exceptionally cruel dogfighting business in his home state of Virginia. As the extent of Vick's cruelty toward the dogs that fought in the enterprise came to light, he became one of the most detested figures in professional sports. He was suspended indefinitely without pay by the NFL, sentenced to 23 months in prison, dropped by his sponsors, and forced into bankruptcy.

Vick missed two NFL seasons while serving his sentence in federal prison and then under house arrest in Virginia. In 2009 the Philadelphia Eagles made the extremely controversial move of signing him to a two-year contract. Vick was a backup quarterback in 2009 and saw little playing time. When the Eagles' first-string quarterback suffered an injury early in the 2010 season, however, Vick stepped into the starter's role with aplomb, leading the Eagles to the National Football Conference (NFC) East division title and posting passing and rushing statistics that placed him among the NFL's top quarterbacks. Likewise, his off-the-field image improved, and he once again became a sought-after product endorser. Questions about whether or not Vick had truly reformed lingered among many in the media and the public, but no one disputed his ability as a player.

"Michael Vick," Gale Biography in Context, *2012.*

Americans love their athletes, and Michael Vick is a talented football player, but he is no better than the man convicted of recreational drug use. However, Vick got his second chance as he should have because he paid his debt to society according to the law. If Vick had been a clerk at Walmart, he would not be given a second chance and the likelihood of him ending up back in prison because of a lack of a job would be all but certain. His crime, although atrocious, certainly did not warrant calls for execution, but if he were not a famous athlete, he may as well have been executed because the rest of his life would have been spent in prison.

Americans are quick to forgive celebrities for their crimes and happy to see them prosper when they are given a second, third, or fourth opportunity to become productive. It is high time that Americans afford the same opportunities to regular citizens who are convicted of crimes whether victimless or not. President Obama has set a precedent that lawmakers should follow by passing legislation that enables every ex-convict the opportunity at a second chance once they have paid their debt to society; although with so much money to be made by keeping the prisons full, that likelihood is remote at best.

| "We are sending a mixed message that it is wrong to commit a crime unless you are a professional athlete."

Professional Sports Leadership Encourages Criminality Among Athletes

Holly Hughes

Holly Hughes is a reporter for the McClatchy newspaper company. In the following viewpoint, she considers the question of whether the commissioners of professional sports leagues are condoning criminal behavior by allowing troubled athletes to continue to play. Hughes argues that the commissioners' refusal to mete out substantial penalties sends a message that such behavior will be tolerated and that elite athletes are above the law. Owners and commissioners share the responsibility of a player's illegal actions, she maintains, and they should realize that they need to change their reactions to players' bad behavior to make it stop.

As you read, consider the following questions:

1. What does Hughes propose to get to the root cause of why some players engage in criminal activities?

2. For what do people say that NFL stands, according to the author?

3. What two NFL players does the author identify as pillars of the community?

In today's age of electronic media, we are immediately made aware of any item considered newsworthy. Many of those items have to do with those in our society who have been raised to the status of hero or role model—movie stars, popular politicians and professional athletes.

When your average Joe is arrested for a felony or a misdemeanor involving violence, it's not always featured in the newspapers or the nightly news. However, when a professional athlete gets arrested, you can be sure the details will be trumpeted far and wide. When that happens, the questions abound. People are outraged that these so-called role models are engaging in this behavior. Others question how someone with so much money would do something so stupid and risk it all.

As a former prosecutor, I can tell you that people from all economic strata do stupid, i.e., criminal, things. The more interesting inquiry to me is this: What is the root cause of the increasing number of professional athletes being arrested for serious crimes? Is it environment or ego?

The Message to Society

Professional athletes have been elevated to the status of role models in our society. Is this hero worship contributing to a wanton disregard of the law by some players? Do these players somehow feel entitled to behave in any manner they wish? Additionally, are the leagues they play in endorsing this behavior by continuing to allow them to play after they have been convicted? There are many professions that exclude convicted felons from being able to continue in their pre-conviction em-

"Sports and Crime," cartoon by John Cole, *The Scranton Times-Tribune*, www.Political
Cartoons.com. Copyright © 2007 by John Cole, www.PoliticalCartoons.com.

ployment. Are the commissioners of pro sports leagues condoning bad behavior by allowing troubled athletes to continue
to play?

It seems to send a message that there are no consequences
to their behavior. Do we really want to send a message to
America's youth that we reward bad behavior? We are sending
a mixed message that it is wrong to commit a crime unless
you are a professional athlete. If Bobo from the block were arrested and charged with the same felonies, he would have a
hard time getting a job at a car wash. Allowing misbehaving
athletes to continue playing after being convicted of a felony
just feeds an ego that they are above the law.

If it is not ego, then is it environment? Did these players
who are being convicted of felonious behavior grow up in
particularly crime-ridden neighborhoods? Are they just continuing in the same behavioral patterns that they have prac-
ticed all their lives? Are they continuing to associate with
childhood friends who draw them into dangerous and ill-

advised schemes and crimes? I don't know the answers to this litany of questions, but perhaps the commissioners of pro leagues should commission a study. If we can get to the root cause of why some players engage in criminal endeavors, perhaps we can put an end to it.

There would be no losers from conducting such a study. If the cause is environmental, the players could be counseled on how to avoid career-threatening pitfalls. They win by avoiding a criminal conviction, their would-be victims win and the reputations of their leagues improve. Their law-abiding fellow players also benefit by not being lumped in with those who break the law. Surely, we have all heard by now that the NFL [National Football League] derisively stands for "National Felons League." Most of us know about the serious legal issues that brought down Philadelphia Eagles quarterback Michael Vick [convicted on dogfighting charges] and New York Jets wide receiver Plaxico Burress [convicted on a gun charge]. Both served highly publicized prison sentences before their recent re-admittances into the NFL.

The NFL

Still, the "National Felons League" moniker is an unfortunate and certainly unfair designation to apply to an entire league of players, many of whom are solid citizens just like the rest of us. And some of them, such as cornerback Nnamdi Asomugha of the Eagles and quarterback Peyton Manning of the Indianapolis Colts [playing with the Denver Broncos as of 2012], are considered to be known pillars of the community.

But on the other side of the ledger, if the cause of misbehavior is ego, then the big bosses need to be willing to address that player's wanton disregard for the law by refusing [him] reentry. While I acknowledge that professional sports is, first and foremost, a business, the owners and commissioners should bear some responsibility for how their young fans view pro athletes.

We often hear that athletes are role models and should comport themselves accordingly. I submit that the owners and commissioners should share in this enormous responsibility. By allowing convicted felons to return, they, too, are sending a bad message to today's fans. It is as irresponsible as putting a knowingly defective product on the market.

If any other business entity had the same number of convicted criminals in their organizations as professional sports teams do, they would be frantically hiring management consultants to address the issue. It's time for owners and commissioners to man up and be responsible for the reputation of their teams and the message they are sending our youth.

Periodical and Internet Sources Bibliography

The following articles have been selected to supplement the diverse views presented in this chapter.

Chris Anderson	"Ethics Thrown Aside: Professional Sports Need a Makeover," *Bleacher Report*, January 25, 2011.
Nick Benas	"Do Top Athletes Deserve Millions? Yes, They Deserve Every Dollar," *Huffington Post*, February 17, 2010.
Erik Brady	"Why Athletes Go Broke: Too Much Spending, Little Liquidity," *USA Today*, April 10, 2012.
Richard Ehrlich	"Why Do Millionaire Entertainers and Athletes Go Broke?," FoxBusiness.com, May 29, 2012.
Daniel J. Flynn	"Split Wide and Disarmed," *American Spectator*, June 15, 2011.
Ron Lieber	"Financial Lessons from Sports Stars' Mistake," *New York Times*, September 9, 2011.
Anthony Riccobono	"Why Do So Many Athletes Go Broke?," *International Business Times*, October 2, 2012.
Ty Schalter	"Why NFL Players Really Go Bankrupt," *Bleacher Report*, May 30, 2012.
Dave Seminara	"New Playbook for Post-Career Success," *New York Times*, January 29, 2012.
Kunbi Tinuoye	"Does 'Baby Mama Drama' Make Pro Athletes Go Broke?," TheGrio.com, April 20, 2012.
Derek Togerson	"Million-Dollar Athletes Go Broke," NBC San Diego, May 17, 2010. www.nbcsandiego.com.

For Further Discussion

Chapter 1

1. Richard Lowe contends that professional athletes are role models. In her viewpoint, Raina Kelley argues that they are not. What is your opinion? Be prepared to defend it.

2. After reading the viewpoints in this chapter, how do you view the role of the media when it comes to depicting professional athletes as role models? How do you think the media can do a better job? Explain.

3. J. Patrick Dobel contends that professional athletes are natural politicians, while Robert Lipsyte argues that athletes make poor politicians. Which author makes the better argument, and why?

Chapter 2

1. Steroids are a controversial issue in sports. In his viewpoint, Charles Leroux asserts that professional athletes should be allowed to use steroids. Reed Albergotti argues that athletes who use steroids should be banned from professional sports for life. With which author do you agree? Explain your reasoning.

2. In recent years, a spotlight has been put on the issue of concussions in professional sports. After reading viewpoints by Jed Hughes, Jon Wertheim, Stu Durando, and Howard Fendrich, offer some suggestions on how sports organizations can better prevent serious head injuries to their players. What two recommendations do you feel could make the biggest difference on the issue? Explain.

Chapter 3

1. Do professional athletes and managers have the right to express controversial opinions? Read viewpoints from Nsenga K. Burton, Cathal Kelly, and Bethlehem Shoals to inform your opinion.

2. Samuel Coffin maintains that professional athletes should not be criticized for public and excessive religious expression. In his viewpoint, Jonathan Zimmerman argues that players should not engage in religious expression. Which author makes the more convincing argument? Explain your reasoning.

3. Many professional athletes are active in social media. In their viewpoints, Lisa Lewis and Thomas van Schaik scrutinize the opportunities and dangers of this trend. What are some of the benefits of social media for professional athletes? What are some of the dangers?

Chapter 4

1. Are professional athletes overpaid or are their salaries justified? Explain your reasoning. Read the viewpoint written by Dan K. Thomasson and conduct additional research online to inform your answer.

2. RMuse contends that professional athletes get preferential treatment when it comes to crime. What factors do you think lead to some athletes getting lighter sentences and preferential treatment? How could society address this issue? Explain.

Organizations to Contact

The editors have compiled the following list of organizations concerned with the issues debated in this book. The descriptions are derived from materials provided by the organizations. All have publications or information available for interested readers. The list was compiled on the date of publication of the present volume; the information provided here may change. Be aware that many organizations take several weeks or longer to respond to inquiries, so allow as much time as possible.

American Civil Liberties Union (ACLU)
125 Broad Street, 18th Floor, New York, NY   10004
(212) 549-2500
website: www.aclu.org

The American Civil Liberties Union (ACLU) is an organization that works to protect and extend the rights of all Americans, particularly First Amendment rights, equal protection under the law, the right to due process, and the right to privacy. The ACLU fights against the thorniest issues such as racism, sexism, homophobia, religious intolerance, and censorship. However, the organization defends individuals and businesses who voice controversial opinions from censorship and values the right of free speech in public, on television and radio, in print, and on the Internet. On its website, the ACLU posts videos, podcasts, games, documents, reports, and speech transcripts, as well news and commentary on censorship and free speech issues. It also offers a blog and in-depth reports on related issues.

Major League Baseball (MLB)
245 Park Avenue, 31st Floor, New York, NY   10167
(212) 931-7800 • fax: (212) 949-5654
website: http://mlb.mlb.com

Major League Baseball (MLB) is the professional baseball league for professional baseball players; it is made up of thirty teams that are split between two leagues. MLB coordinates and determines the schedule of regular and play-off games; organizes the annual all-star game and associated activities; hires umpires and other support staff; works with broadcast networks, radio, and other media outlets to broadcast games; markets teams, leagues, and players; negotiates policies and enforces regulations; and works with team owners on a wide range of issues to maintain a financially successful professional baseball league in the United States. The MLB website offers access to information on the league's philanthropic initiatives, press releases, a guide to the rules of the game, and wireless products and services, as well as statistics and standings of teams and players.

Major League Baseball Players Association (MLBPA)
12 East Forty-Ninth Street, 24th Floor, New York, NY   10017
(212) 826-0808 • fax: (212) 752-4378
e-mail: feedback@mlbpa.org
website: http://mlbplayers.mlb.com

The Major League Baseball Players Association (MLBPA) is the labor union for professional baseball players in Major League Baseball (MLB). It acts as the collective bargaining agent for current players in contract negotiations and salary arbitrations with the MLB. The MLBPA also "works closely with MLB in ensuring that the playing conditions for all games involving Major League players, whether the games are played in MLB stadiums or elsewhere, including internationally, meet proper safety guidelines." Another of its key responsibilities is as group licensing agent on behalf of the players. Recent video of players and breaking news, as well as other relevant information, can be found on the MLBPA website.

National Basketball Association (NBA)
645 Fifth Avenue, New York, NY   10022
(212) 407-8000
website: www.nba.com

The National Basketball Association (NBA) is the professional basketball league in the United States and Canada. The NBA coordinates the regular and play-off game schedules for the thirty teams that make up the league; organizes the annual all-star game and associated activities; negotiates contracts with broadcast networks, radio, and other media outlets to broadcast games; innovatively and aggressively markets teams, leagues, and players through community outreach programs and other initiatives; enforces league rules and hires and manages league officials; and works with team owners on a wide range of issues to maintain a financially successful professional basketball league in the United States. The NBA website has the league's schedule, statistics, player blogs, videos, mobile apps, photos, and other features.

National Basketball Players Association (NBPA)
310 Lenox Avenue, New York, NY 10027
(212) 655-0880 • fax: (212) 655-0881
e-mail: info@nbpa.com
website: www.nbpa.com

The National Basketball Players Association (NBPA) represents the interests of National Basketball Association (NBA) players. Its responsibilities include negotiating the terms of a collective bargaining agreement (CBA) with the NBA; certifying, regulating, and educating player agents; providing a full range of services, benefits, and assistance through its own focused NBPA department, Player Services; and performing public relations to promote players and the game in the community and in the media. The NBPA website offers a range of information on NBA activities and breaking news, photos, videos, and updates on philanthropic efforts all over the world.

National Football League (NFL)
345 Park Avenue, New York, NY 10017
(212) 450-2000
website: www.nfl.com

The National Football League (NFL) is the premier professional league for football in the United States. The league consists of thirty-two teams split between two conferences—the American Football Conference (AFC) and the National Football Conference (NFC). The NFL performs myriad tasks such as scheduling and coordinating preseason, regular season, and play-off game series; formulating, monitoring, and enforcing rules and setting policy on all relevant fronts; negotiating contracts with television, radio, and other media outlets for broadcast of NFL games; licensing and merchandising products; and working closely with team owners on a wide range of issues to maintain a safe, profitable, and exciting level of competition. The NFL website offers information on players, teams, fantasy football, and league history; features podcasts, videos, blogs, and many other features; and provides a community for NFL fans to discuss teams, players, and plays in fan forums.

National Football League Players Association (NFLPA)
2021 L Street NW, Washington, DC   20036
(202) 463-2200
website: www.nflplayers.com

The National Football League Players Association (NFLPA) acts as the labor union for the players of the National Football League (NFL), representing players in all negotiations regarding the collective bargaining agreement (CBA) and monitoring retirement and insurance benefits. The issue of head injuries and concussions is very important to the NFLPA, and the organization lobbies for more research and better policies for players when it comes to injuries. The NFLPA also protects the rights of players by appealing disciplinary measures imposed by the NFL and promotes the image of players across the league through public relations campaigns. The NFLPA website offers a wealth of photos, statistics on individual players, videos, blogs, and the latest news from the NFL.

National Hockey League (NHL)
1185 Sixth Avenue, New York, NY   10036
(212) 789-2000
website: www.nhl.com

Founded in 1917, the National Hockey League (NHL) is the top league for professional ice hockey in the United States and

Canada. The NHL operates a league of thirty hockey clubs with players from more than twenty countries around the world. As with any professional sports league, the NHL performs a wide range of jobs, including scheduling and managing preseason, regular season, and play-off game series; making, revising, and enforcing rules and imposing discipline on players who break those rules; setting policy on a number of issues, including the best ways to deal with concussions and other player injuries; negotiating contracts with television, radio, and other media outlets for broadcast of NHL games; licensing and merchandising products; and working closely with team owners on a wide range of issues to maintain a safe, profitable, and exciting level of competition on the ice. The official NHL website includes features, news, rosters, statistics, schedules, teams, live game radio broadcasts, and video clips.

National Hockey League Players' Association (NHLPA)

20 Bay Street, Suite 1700, Toronto, ON   M5J 2N8
  Canada
website: www.nhlpa.com

The National Hockey League Players' Association (NHLPA) was established in 1967 as the labor union for the professional hockey players in the National Hockey League (NHL). The NHLPA works to protect the rights of professional players and represent them in negotiations under the collective bargaining agreement (CBA). One of its key missions is to work on behalf of players when it comes to researching, treating, and recovering from injuries. The NHLPA also supports numerous philanthropic efforts, including "Hockey Fights Cancer" and "Hockey for Haiti." The NHLPA website offers a wealth of information on players, statistics, topical issues, and breaking news. It also provides access to a range of videos and a Twitter board, which lists tweets from active NHL players.

Women's National Basketball Association (WNBA)
645 Fifth Avenue, New York, NY 10022
website: www.wnba.com

The Women's National Basketball Association (WNBA) was established in 1996 by the National Basketball Association (NBA) as a professional league for female basketball players. Currently, the league is composed of thirteen professional teams. The WNBA manages a full schedule of regular and play-off games; negotiates with broadcast networks, radio, and other media outlets to broadcast games; markets teams, leagues, and players through community outreach programs; formulates effective policies and enforces regulations; and works with team owners on a wide range of issues to maintain a financially successful professional women's basketball league in the United States.

Bibliography of Books

John Amaechi — *Man in the Middle*. New York: ESPN Books, 2007.

Ben Carrington — *Race, Sport and Politics: The Sporting Black Diaspora*. London: SAGE, 2010.

Linda Carroll and David Rosner — *The Concussion Crisis: Anatomy of a Silent Epidemic*. New York: Simon & Schuster, 2012.

Paul Christesen — *Sport and Democracy in the Ancient and Modern Worlds*. New York: Cambridge University Press, 2012.

Gay Culverhouse — *Throwaway Players: The Concussion Crisis: From Pee Wee Football to the NFL*. Lake Forest, CA: Behler Publications, 2012.

Gerald L. Early — *A Level Playing Field: African American Athletes and the Republic of Sports*. Cambridge, MA: Harvard University Press, 2011.

Curtis Eichelberger — *Men of Sunday: How Faith Guides the Players, Coaches, and Wives of the NFL*. Nashville, TN: Thomas Nelson, 2012.

Stephen G. Gordon — *Tim Tebow: Quarterback with Conviction*. Minneapolis, MN: Twenty-First Century Books, 2013.

Declan Hill — *The Fix: Soccer and Organized Crime*. Plattsburgh, NY: McClelland & Stewart, 2010.

Abraham Iqbal Khan

Curt Flood in the Media: Baseball, Race, and the Demise of the Activist-Athlete. Jackson: University Press of Mississippi, 2012.

Bob Latham

Winners & Losers: Rants, Riffs & Reflections on the World of Sports. Austin, TX: Greenleaf Book Group, 2012.

David J. Leonard

After Artest: The NBA and the Assault on Blackness. Albany: State University of New York Press, 2012.

Robert Lipsyte

An Accidental Sportswriter: A Memoir. New York: Ecco, 2011.

Amy Jo Martin

Renegades Write the Rules: How the Digital Royalty Use Social Media to Innovate. San Francisco, CA: Jossey-Bass, 2012.

Rick Morrissey

Ozzie's School of Management: Lessons from the Dugout, the Clubhouse, and the Doghouse. New York: Times Books, 2012.

Christopher Nowinski

Head Games: Football's Concussion Crisis from the NFL to Youth Leagues. East Bridgewater, MA: Drummond Publishing Group, 2007.

Roy Simmons

Out of Bounds: Coming Out of Sexual Abuse, Addiction, and My Life of Lies in the NFL Closet. New York: Carroll & Graf, 2006.

Tim Tebow with   *Through My Eyes: A Quarterback's*
Nathan Whitaker   *Journey.* Grand Rapids, MI:
                  Zondervan, 2011.

Stanley H.   *Athletes Who Indulge Their Dark Side:*
Teitelbaum   *Sex, Drugs, and Cover-Ups.* Santa
                  Barbara, CA: Praeger, 2010.

Brian Tuohy   *The Fix Is In: The Showbiz*
                  Manipulations of the NFL, MLB,
                  NBA, NHL and NASCAR. Port
                  Townsend, WA: Feral House, 2010.

Mike Yorkey   *Playing with Purpose: Tim Tebow.*
                  Uhrichsville, OH: Barbour
                  Publishers, 2012.

Kevin Young   *Sport, Violence and Society.* New York:
                  Routledge, 2012.

Andrew Zimbalist *Circling the Bases: Essays on the*
                  Challenges and Prospects of the Sports
                  Industry. Philadelphia, PA: Temple
                  University Press, 2011.

Andrew Zimbalist *In the Best Interests of Baseball?:*
                  Governing the National Pastime.
                  Lincoln: University of Nebraska
                  Press, 2013.

Index

CPSIA information can be obtained
at www.ICGtesting.com
Printed in the USA
FFOW05n1645221013